THE
PROMISE
OF PROVISION

Books by Derek Prince

THE
PROMISE
OF PROVISION

LIVING AND GIVING
FROM GOD'S
ABUNDANT SUPPLY

DEREK PRINCE

Chosen
a division of Baker Publishing Group
Minneapolis, Minnesota

This book was compiled from the extensive archive of Derek Prince's unpublished materials and edited by the Derek Prince Ministries editorial team.

Published by Chosen Books
11400 Hampshire Avenue South
Bloomington, Minnesota 55438
www.chosenbooks.com

Chosen Books is a division of
Baker Publishing Group, Grand Rapids, Michigan

Printed in the United States of America

Library of Congress Cataloging-in-Publication Data

Prince, Derek.
    The promise of provision : living and giving from God's abundant supply /
Derek Prince.
        p.   cm.
    Includes index.
    ISBN 978-0-8007-9522-1 (pbk. : alk. paper)
    1. Wealth—Religious aspects—Christianity. 2. Providence and government of
God—Christianity. I. Title.
    BR115.W4P745 2011
    231'.5—dc23   2011026291

14 15 16 17   7 6 5 4 3 2

Contents

Introduction

Provision, abundance and *prosperity* are loaded terms in the world's vernacular today, and especially so in most Christian circles. If you were to ask any believer in Jesus Christ what comes to mind at the mention of these terms, the wide variety of responses you would receive might be amazing to you. In fact, those responses would probably include more than a few heated and reactionary remarks.

The truth is that the topics of prosperity and abundance have sparked a great deal of distorted and imbalanced teaching in the attention given to them. The spectrum ranges from the extremes of "the prosperity gospel" and "name-it-and-claim-it" proponents to the view held by many devout believers that poverty is a virtue and a sign of deep spirituality.

Which is correct? Is there validity somewhere between the boundaries of the two extremes? Is there a balanced approach to be found? Christians need solidity and balance in this area because, in many instances, tremendous confusion has been loosed upon the Christian community. Regrettably, from the world's viewpoint, great dishonor has also come to the Church because of our ambivalence and ignorance about the purpose of God's provision as well as our use (and frequent abuse) of financial resources.

Would you agree that we all need balanced teaching from the Word of God to help us find our moorings in this sensitive area?

Check yourself out on this matter. Have you struggled in your own experience to find equilibrium in regard to the use of God's resources? Have you asked questions like the ones that follow?

- Is wealth a worldly temptation or a useful tool?
- Is poverty a blessing or a curse?
- Have I been jaundiced by a distorted view of prosperity?
- Am I properly stewarding what God has given me?
- Is my attitude toward finances pleasing to Him?
- Have I installed material acquisition as a goal in my life?
- If so, what is my motivation for seeking abundant resources?
- What is the real purpose for the resources God has given me?

These are just a few of the questions that easily come to mind when we are addressing the matter of God's provision and abundance. Frankly, it is absolutely appropriate to ask ourselves the hard questions. Indeed, it is especially healthy to do so in the context of some down-to-earth, practical teaching from the Word of God.

Enter *The Promise of Provision* by Derek Prince. We believe you will find this book refreshing, enlightening and, we hope, life-altering. Let us say right up front, however, that this book is not intended to be the last word regarding abundance. As helpful as it will be for you, we don't regard it as "the ultimate or final word" on how you should regard and steward the resources God provides. Much helpful material in the way of manuals and instruction books has already been published on these topics. A great deal of that information is certainly worthy of your ongoing attention and consideration.

But if you are looking for one volume that will give you clear insight, a reasoned approach, renewed motivation to handle resources properly and a solid biblical foundation in this important area, you are holding the right book in your hands.

One signature trait of all of Derek Prince's teaching during his sixty years of ministry (he passed away in 2003) was his resolute focus on the Bible as the authoritative source of guiding principles for life and experience. We have drawn from the archives of Derek's teaching on the topic of finances and abundance to give you an encouraging and helpful resource. We believe it will allow you to clear away some of the fog you may have encountered in this area of your life.

For example, here are some unique categories Derek's teaching offers in the book you are about to read:

- Clear definitions of what abundance is and what it is not
- An enlightening perspective on "prosperity" in the ministry of Paul
- The reality of "the poverty curse" and how to be released from it
- The amazing exchange that Jesus accomplished on the cross
- The clear promises of the Bible regarding God's provision for us
- The conditions we must meet to walk faithfully in this arena
- A grasp of the real reasons God gives us resources
- How to put your finances to practical and fruitful use
- Our mandate to invest God's provision in people

You may not agree with everything Derek has stated in this book. In fact, what you read here may stimulate further thinking and spark some additional questions for you to consider. (That's actually a good result of reading any book.)

But here are a few results we can promise if you read this book through to the end. First, you will be enlightened by what you have learned. Second, you will have a much better grasp of what the Bible mandates for you in this important, yet sensitive area you have to handle. Third, you will be equipped with some clear guidelines and action steps for improving your use of the resources God gives you—not only in the present, but far into the future as well. Fourth, and possibly most importantly, you will be motivated by a renewed vision and commitment to the steps God expects you to take in the world around you with the abundance He provides.

In the final analysis, when we ultimately stand before the Lord to give an account of our stewardship here on earth, each of us wants to be in a position to hear the Lord say, "Well done, good and faithful servant. Enter into the joy of your Master" (Matthew 25:23, RSV).

Our prayer is that *The Promise of Provision* by Derek Prince will help to better prepare you for that eternal moment.

The International Publishing Team
of Derek Prince Ministries

PART 1

UNDERSTANDING
ABUNDANCE

1

From Pardon to Provision

One distinctive aspect of God, as He is revealed in the Bible, is His *abundance*. God is not poor. He is not stingy. He is not limited. He is a God of *abundance*. His grace is abundant. His love is abundant. His provision is abundant. If we are to represent God accurately to the world around us—the way He really is—then we must learn to represent Him as a God of *abundance*.

Two portions of Scripture from the book of Jeremiah help us grasp what God wants us to understand regarding His abundance—and they also help us see why we are often far removed from receiving it. In the first Scripture, we learn that in order to comprehend God's abundance, we must first acknowledge the depth of our need. In Jeremiah 30, God shows Israel the abysmal depth of their own need. These words are addressed to the people of Israel, to their land and to the city of Jerusalem:

> "For thus says the LORD: 'Your affliction is incurable, your wound is severe. There is no one to plead your cause, that you may be bound up; you have no healing medicines. All your lovers have forgotten you; they do not seek you; for I have wounded you with the wound of an enemy, with the chastisement of a cruel one, for the multitude of your iniquities, because your sins have increased.'"
>
> Jeremiah 30:12–14

As always, God speaks very plainly to His people. He says, "Your condition is hopeless." The King James Version of the Bible says, "Thy bruise is incurable, and thy wound is grievous." And God states very plainly the reason for this situation: "Because your sins have increased."

In other words, the consequence of sin, ultimately, is misery, poverty and destitution. There is no abundance in a life of sin, and there is no source to which they can look for help because there is no one who can help them.

But God does not leave us there. He offers both pardon and provision. In Jeremiah 33, God promises the help that He alone can give, having first excluded all human sources of help. Speaking again to His people Israel, to their land and to the city of Jerusalem, God says:

> "Behold, I will bring it health and healing; I will heal them and reveal to them the abundance of peace and truth. And I will cause the captives of Judah and the captives of Israel to return, and will rebuild those places as at the first. I will cleanse them from all their iniquity by which they have sinned against Me, and I will pardon all their iniquities by which they have sinned and by which they have transgressed against Me."
>
> Jeremiah 33:6–8

That is God's remedy for a situation that He has declared to be incurable. But, of course, when He says it is incurable, He is excepting Himself. God is able to cure that which man cannot cure.

As always, God's diagnosis goes right to the root of the problem. He says, "Your sin has to be dealt with. When you are cleansed from your sin and your rebellion is pardoned, then I can help you." And He says in this connection, "I will bring it health and healing; I will heal them and reveal to them the abundance of peace and truth. And I will cause the captives . . . to return, and will rebuild those places as at the first."

We see here three related purposes of God in His promise of abundance. The first is *restoration*. Restoration is a sovereign act of God on behalf of His people—giving back that which sin has robbed from them. Out of restoration comes *revelation*. Finally, out of revelation comes *abundance*.

Understanding God's Thinking

We are living in a season when God is restoring His people—both Israel and the Church of Jesus Christ. In the process of that restoration comes His revelation, and out of His revelation, we can once again apprehend His abundance that we had lost sight of through our sin and rebellion. I want to focus for a moment on His revelation, for this is the way we understand God's purposes in all that He provides.

This revelation comes only from the Word of God through the Spirit of God. Paul emphasizes this principle in 1 Corinthians: "However, as it is written: 'No eye has seen, no ear has heard, no mind has conceived what God has prepared for those who love him'" (1 Corinthians 2:9, NIV).

What God has prepared for His people cannot be apprehended by the natural senses or the natural reasoning of man. Those abilities are excluded. The alternative is then stated in the next verse:

> God has revealed it to us by his Spirit. The [Holy] Spirit searches all things, even the deep things of God. For who among men knows the thoughts of a man except the man's spirit within him? In the same way no one knows the thoughts of God except the Spirit of God.
>
> verses 10–11, NIV

The only way we can understand God's thinking and God's purposes is through the revelation of God's Spirit. Then Paul goes on to make a really dramatic statement: "We have not received the spirit of the world but the Spirit who is from God, that we may understand what God has freely given us" (verse 12, NIV).

This awareness guides us as we study the theme of abundance—the fact that we can understand what God has freely given to us, and that this is only understood by the Holy Spirit. Paul goes on: "This is what we speak, not in words taught us by human wisdom but in words taught by the Spirit, expressing spiritual truths in spiritual words" (verse 13, NIV).

Not merely is the truth from the Spirit, but the words that adequately express the truth must also be given by the Spirit. We must learn God's terminology. Paul affirms what we saw earlier—that the natural man, no matter how educated or sophisticated, cannot appreciate these truths.

> The man without the Spirit [the Greek means "the natural, or the soulish, one—the one who relies on his own soulish understanding"] does not accept the things that come from the Spirit of God, for they are foolishness to him, and he cannot understand them, because they are spiritually discerned.
>
> verse 14, NIV

Let me emphasize again that receiving revelation depends on opening up to the Spirit of God. Apart from the Spirit of God there is no possibility to get this revelation.

One Supreme Purpose for Abundance

Paul then ends with some marvelous words:

> The spiritual man makes judgments about all things, but he himself is not subject to any man's judgment: "For who has known the mind of the Lord that he may instruct him?" But we have the mind of Christ.
>
> verses 15–16, NIV

That is a dramatic statement. Through the Holy Spirit we can receive the mind of Christ. With the mind of Christ we can appreciate all that God has freely given to us. We can apprehend His abundance. And God's abundance is revealed and made available to us for one supreme purpose—not for human satisfaction, but for God's glory.

In Jeremiah 33:9, after His promise of restoration and abundance, God says:

"It shall be to Me a name of joy, a praise, and an honor before all nations of the earth, who shall hear all the good that I do to them; they shall fear and tremble for all the goodness and all the prosperity that I provide for it."

God has presented a picture of His people, His land and His city—captive and hopeless, desolate and ruined. He has told them that the condition is incurable. Then, out of His grace and His sovereignty, He promises restoration. Then, out of restoration, revelation. And out of revelation, abundance.

Then He says, in effect, "When I have done this, it will bring glory to Me. The completed work of restoration will be to Me a name of joy, a praise and an honor before all the nations of the earth, who shall hear of all the good that I do to them. And they [all the nations of the earth] shall fear and tremble for all the goodness and all the prosperity that I provide for it."

It impresses me deeply that God's purpose is to restore to His people such abundance, such prosperity, such manifest demonstration of His goodness that all the other peoples of the earth will fear and tremble to see it. That is the level of God's abundance.

In the first part of this book, I will focus on basic spiritual truths that help us understand God's supernatural provision for us. We will learn how to break free from a poverty spirit and see that God gives us an abundance for every good work.

Then in succeeding parts I will explain the principles, steps and conditions for receiving God's abundance. These provide practical guidelines, which, when followed, allow for God's generous Kingdom blessings.

In the final part, we will study the purpose for which God gives us abundance.

In connection with the restoration of Israel, God states, "I will . . . reveal to them the abundance of peace and truth." God longs for you to have fruitfulness in every area of your life. In fact, He has already provided everything you need—plus more! God is a God of abundance. I pray that He will grant that revelation to you as you read.

Abundance Defined

It is very important that we understand precisely the meaning of God's provision. Does it mean great material wealth? Does it mean enough to get by? What exactly does God's provision include?

We will be answering this question throughout this part of the book, but let me begin by examining some of the basic words or concepts that I use in this connection. They are all interrelated, but not all synonymous, having different shades of meaning. There are four main words on the positive side of provision:

riches
wealth
prosperity
abundance

One important distinction within these positive concepts is that when we use the words *riches* or *wealth*, we are speaking about considerable financial or material assets. These words imply that a person has large sums of money, owns large properties and other valuables. But when we speak about *prosperity* and *abundance*, the implication is not necessarily that a person has a lot of money in the bank or owns great material possessions. God's promise is primarily that we have prosperity and abundance rather than riches and wealth.

There are three main words on the negative side. I would suggest the following:

> *poverty*
>
> *want*
>
> *failure*

Abundance and prosperity, then, suggest something that is the opposite of poverty, want and failure.

True Success

In short, when we think in terms of God's provision, when we look at the concept of living in abundance and prosperity, we are not necessarily talking about people whom the world would classify as being very wealthy or rich. Rather, we are thinking in terms of succeeding in what each individual is commissioned to do. Let me show you what I mean from two Scriptures.

In his third epistle, John says, "Beloved, I pray that you may prosper in all things and be in health, just as your soul prospers" (3 John 2). What a beautiful statement of the will of God for the committed believer! Gaius, to whom the epistle was written, was a model believer. If you study the epistle, you will find that he was walking in all the truth that God had made available; and the apostle John, writing as the mouthpiece of the Holy Spirit, said to him, "Beloved, I pray that you may *prosper* in all things and be in *health,* just as your *soul prospers.*" This covers all areas of life—including the material. In every one of them the will of God is good!

The word translated "prosper" here means literally "to have a prosperous or successful journey or accomplish what you intend to do successfully." In Romans 1:10, Paul is praying that he may "have a prosperous journey by the will of God" (KJV) to visit the Christians at Rome. It is the same word. Scripture reveals that God answered Paul's prayer. His journey to Rome is described in Acts 27–28.

You will notice from the description of that "prosperous journey," however, that Paul did not travel first class but as a prisoner in chains. He went through a tremendous storm, which lasted about two weeks without ceasing, and it seemed as if the whole ship and all who were on it would be lost. But—through God's intervention—they survived the storm and no one on the ship was lost. They were thrown onto an island as castaways, and when Paul was gathering sticks to make a fire, a viper bit him and hung onto his hand. But the supernatural power of God kept him from any harm. And after that, there was a tremendous move of the Spirit of God on that island (which proved to be Malta). When they left, the islanders loaded them down with all they needed for the rest of their journey.

And so, ultimately, Paul arrived at Rome. He had a prosperous journey, but it was not a comfortable or luxurious journey. It was prosperous because he accomplished God's purpose, which was much higher than human purpose would have been.

Living at a Higher Level

Essentially, *abundance* means you have all you need, plus you have something to spare. Abundance suggests that you are lifted above the level of your own needs and thus are able to reach out to the needs of others.

Let me give you just a little, simple example from daily life. Suppose a woman goes to the grocery store and she needs fifty dollars' worth of groceries. If she only has forty dollars with her, she is shopping out of insufficiency. If she has precisely fifty dollars with her, she is shopping out of sufficiency. But suppose she has sixty dollars with her and she needs fifty dollars' worth of groceries. Then she is shopping out of abundance. She has all that she needs and something left over. Even though it may not be a large amount left over, that is abundance.

When we look again at the four different concepts of provision, we see that the words *riches* and *wealth* are basically synonymous, but they are very different from *prosperity*, which relates to doing something successfully. We see further that *abundance* means that you are not living in poverty—in want or lack or frustration—even though you may not have a great surplus nor even have anything in your bank account.

I always say about Jesus during the period of His earthly ministry that He did not have a big bank account (although He and His disciples did have a bag into which they deposited offerings). Rather He simply relied upon His Father's "credit," and it was always honored.

Actually, *very* wealthy people really do not require a lot of cash. I was with a wealthy man once in a restaurant and he provided a beautiful meal for me. At the end, he never even produced a card. He just signed his name on the bill. That was enough, because they knew it would be taken care of.

Was Jesus Poor?

Jesus, in His earthly ministry, exemplified abundance. Many people fail to see this. They picture Jesus as being poor throughout His life, but in the truest sense He was not poor. He had abundance.

He did not have large amounts of cash or material possessions, but He had abundance.

He had nowhere to lay His head, but He had abundance. He depended on others to provide Him with a sleeping place, yet He was never without one.

He was able to feed about twelve thousand people—men, women and children—with five loaves and two fishes. That is not poverty. Actually, Jesus had much more left over after feeding those twelve thousand persons than He had when He started (see Matthew 14:15–21). What a beautiful picture of abundance!

Another time when the question arose about His need to pay tax, instead of sending Peter to the bank with a check, He sent Peter to the Sea of Galilee with a fish hook and said, "Just cast in your fish hook—don't put bait on it, just cast the hook in—and take up the first fish that comes. Open its mouth and you'll find the tax money." That is an unorthodox way to pay your taxes, but Jesus used this method to meet the need.

Remarkably enough, Jesus imparted His same attitude to His disciples. When He sent them out, He said, "Freely you have received; freely give" (Matthew 10:8). He did not send them out to get; He sent them out to give. That is the essence of abundance. Its ultimate expression is giving.

Afterward, right near the end of His ministry, Jesus checked on what the disciples had experienced when He had sent them out. The record says: "[Jesus] said to them, 'When I sent you without money bag, knapsack, and sandals, did you lack anything?' So they said, 'Nothing'" (Luke 22:35).

That is abundance. They did not have a lot of equipment or spare clothes. They did not carry a bag with money in it, yet they did not lack anything. And they gave freely out of what Jesus had imparted to them. It is important to see that you can have abundance without being wealthy by this world's standards.

As we consider abundance, let's take our focus away from the idea of having a lot of money in the bank. *Abundance* does not necessarily indicate possessions of large sums of money or property. But it does suggest something that is the opposite of poverty, want and failure.

3

Blessings from Following God

The realization that God is the source of all provision leads us to a basic principle that is emphasized consistently throughout Scripture: *Obedience to God brings blessings—abundance in every area of our lives. Disobedience to God brings curses—poverty in every area of our lives.* If we desire to walk in the abundance God desires for us, we need to understand the essential requirements of obedience.

We begin by looking at the Bible's comprehensive list of God's covenant blessings. This is found in Deuteronomy 28:1–14. We will observe the conditions for receiving these blessings, which logically, as usual with God, are stated in the first two verses. In our next chapter, we will observe the list of curses from Deuteronomy 28:15–68.

Two Requirements of Obedience

Here are the two opening verses of Deuteronomy 28:

> "Now it shall be, if you diligently obey the LORD your God, being careful to do all His commandments which I command

you today, the LORD your God will set you high above all the nations of the earth. All these blessings will come upon you and overtake you if you obey the LORD your God."

Deuteronomy 28:1–2, NASB

Twice there, Moses uses the phrase *obey the LORD your God.* It is important to understand that in the original Hebrew, the phrase is a little more elaborate. It is: "Listen to the voice of the LORD your God," and I prefer that translation.

Thus, Moses begins, "If you will diligently listen to the voice of the LORD your God, being careful to do His commandments." Then he ends up again at the end of verse 2, "If you will listen to the voice of the LORD your God."

So the two conditions there for entering into the covenant blessings of God are: first, listening carefully to God's voice; and second, doing what God says. Conversely, we see in verse 15, which opens the listing of curses, that disobedience begins with precisely the opposite: "If thou wilt not hearken unto the voice of the LORD thy God" (KJV). Here, then, is the point at which the two paths divide. The path to all blessings begins when we listen to God's voice; the path to all curses begins when we do not listen to God's voice.

Let me show you two other passages. In Jeremiah 7 the Lord speaks through the prophet to remind Israel what He originally required of them when He brought them out of Egypt. This is what He says (and it is somewhat surprising):

"For I did not speak to your fathers, or command them in the day that I brought them out of the land of Egypt, concerning burnt offerings and sacrifices. [God says, "I wasn't primarily interested in burnt offerings and sacrifices—there was something else that came first." What was it?] But this is what I commanded them, saying, 'Obey My voice, and I will be your God, and you will be My people; and you will walk in all the way which I command you, that it may be well with you.'"

Jeremiah 7:22–23, NASB

That really is God's basic requirement in all ages and dispensations—"Obey My voice and I will be your God." That implies a direct personal relationship with God, because a voice is something personal. We have to be able to hear God's voice before we can obey it. If we do not hear God's voice, it is impossible to obey it.

Now you might say, "That changed in the New Testament." But really it did not. This principle is carried over, unchanged. Read what Jesus Himself says in John 10:27: "My sheep hear My voice, and I know them, and they follow Me" (NASB).

"My sheep . . . My true disciples," Jesus says—and by that, He is not talking about denominations or church groups. "My sheep, all My true disciples." What is the first requirement? "They hear My voice." And second, "They follow Me." That has never changed all through Scripture.

The first requirement is to listen diligently to the voice of the Lord. The second is to do what He says. It is logical to put those requirements in that order, because if you do not hear God's voice you cannot even begin to do what He says.

The Blessings of Provision

Now, let's go back to Deuteronomy 28 and look at the list of blessings for obedience. I am going to pick out some of them. I really recommend to you to read Deuteronomy 28:1–14, and study these blessings carefully. Your careful study will be rewarding to you.

> "And all these blessings shall come upon you and overtake you, because you obey the voice of the LORD your God: Blessed shall you be in the city, and blessed shall you be in the country. Blessed shall be the fruit of your body, the produce of your ground and the increase of your herds, the increase of your cattle and the offspring of your flocks. Blessed shall be your basket and your kneading bowl. . . . The LORD will command the blessing on you in your storehouses and in all to which you set your hand,

and He will bless you in the land. . . . And the LORD will grant you plenty of goods, in the fruit of your body, in the increase of your livestock, and in the produce of your ground. . . . The LORD will open to you His good treasure, the heavens, to give the rain to your land in its season, and to bless all the work of your hand."

verses 2–5, 8, 11–12

Notice the all-inclusive phrases that are used: "*all* to which you set your hand . . . *all* the work of your hand." I want to point out to you briefly the blessings that come from hearing and obeying God's voice.

Verse 1: "The LORD your God will set you high above all the nations of the earth." You will be set high above—you will never be below.

Verse 3: "Blessed shall you be in the city, and blessed shall you be in the country." You will be blessed wherever you go.

Verse 4: "Blessed shall be the fruit of your body, the produce of your ground and the increase of your herds, the increase of your cattle and the offspring of your flocks." This is fruitfulness in every area of your life.

Verse 5: "Blessed shall be your basket and your kneading bowl." Your work preparing food will be blessed.

Verse 6: "Blessed shall you be when you come in, and blessed shall you be when you go out." There is no part of your daily walk that will not be blessed—whether it is going out or coming in.

Verse 7: "The LORD will cause your enemies who rise against you to be defeated before your face; they shall come out against you one way and flee before you seven ways." I often remind the devil of that. "You came out against me one way but you are going to flee from me seven ways" because the blessing gives victory over our enemies.

Verse 8: "The LORD will command the blessing on you in your storehouses and in all to which you set your hand." Everything you do will be blessed.

Verse 9: "The LORD will establish you as a holy people to Himself." Holiness is one of the blessings that flow.

Verse 10: "All peoples of the earth shall see that you are called by the name of the LORD, and they shall be afraid of you." The blessing of the Lord will be manifest, something that people can see, and it will cause them to develop a very special attitude toward you.

Verse 11 is particularly appropriate to our theme of God's abundance: "The LORD will make you abound in prosperity" (NASB). Abundant prosperity is one of the covenant blessings of the Lord. Let's lay hold of that fact.

Verse 12: "The LORD will open to you His good treasure, the heavens, to give the rain to your land in its season, and to bless all the work of your hand." This speaks about the climate and the weather. The verse continues: "You shall lend to many nations, but you shall not borrow." If you do not have to borrow but are in a position to lend, that speaks of financial abundance.

There is an important verse about borrowing and lending in the book of Proverbs: "The rich rules over the poor, and the borrower becomes the lender's slave" (Proverbs 22:7, NASB). Many Christians need to adjust their faith in this area. They have not seen that it is a blessing to lend, but it is not a blessing to have to borrow. They do not realize it, but by being in debt they are in servitude, because the borrower is servant to the lender. The person or institution that lends the money calls the shots. The one who has borrowed is subject to him. And we see here that God's blessing on His people is that we should be the ones who lend and not borrow.

The same all-inclusive phraseology of these verses is repeated in Deuteronomy 29:9: "Therefore keep the words of this covenant, and do them, that you may prosper in all that you do."

The blessings promised are in exact proportion to the obedience required. Total obedience brings total blessing. No area of our lives is excluded. No room is left for failure, for frustration or defeat; there is no room for anything but success.

At the end of the list, as at the beginning, the conditions are plainly stated—listen and do.

"The LORD will make you the head and not the tail, and you only will be above, and you will not be underneath, if you listen [notice we always come back to the condition] to the commandments of the LORD your God, which I charge you today, to observe them carefully [listen and do], and do not turn aside from any of the words which I command you today, to the right or to the left, to go after other gods to serve them."

Deuteronomy 28:13–14, NASB

I think the thirteenth verse beautifully sums up the expression or the outworking of the blessing of God in our lives. The Lord says He will make you the head and not the tail. You will be above and not underneath.

Imagine the following conversation between two Christians. One says to the other, "How are you today, brother?"

And the second one replies, "Under the circumstances, I'm not doing badly."

And the first one says, "Well, what are you doing under the circumstances? You shouldn't be under the circumstances. You're supposed to be above—not underneath."

This Scripture says, "The LORD will make you the head and not the tail." God made this very vivid to me at a certain point. What is the difference between the head and the tail? The head makes the decisions and sets the course. The tail just follows wherever the head goes. When I realized that, I asked myself, *Which am I in my life right now? Am I the head? Do I make the decisions? Or am I the tail? Do I just get pulled around by situations and circumstances over which I have no control?*

That is a decision. Which are you? How are you living today? Are you living like the head or are you living like the tail? Are you under the circumstances or are you above them?

I sometimes shock people, but I say this in sincerity. As a believing servant of the Lord, when I go to buy something that

I believe is God's will for me to have, I don't ask, "Can I afford it?" I ask, "Is this what God wants me to have?" Many times I have discovered that God wants me to have something better than I would have chosen for myself.

Somebody once made a statement that I want to share with you: "God gives His best to those who leave the choice to Him." You see, God cares for us and understands us and loves us better than we ourselves. If we could only trust Him! If we could only come to the place where we walk in close, intimate fellowship with Him, where we listen to His voice and do what He says! As we do, the blessings will take care of themselves.

The Sum of Blessings

Let me recommend to you sincerely that you go back to Deuteronomy 28:1–14 and read those blessings. I am going to sum them up in my own way in just a few words, but I would like you to check for yourself. This is my summation of the blessings:

Exaltation
Health
Fruitfulness
Prosperity
Victory
God's Favor

Who would not want to receive those blessings of God's provision? I don't know about you, but let me say, I want them. And I am willing to try to meet the conditions to receive them.

How Curses Affect Our Lives

It is unrealistic to dwell on the blessings and act as if there were no such things as curses—because they are very real. One fact the Bible makes clear, and that most people do not fully grasp, is that a curse can affect our lives. And clearly, a curse comes for a reason. This is stated decisively in Proverbs 26:2: "Like a sparrow in its flitting, like a swallow in its flying, so a curse without cause does not alight" (NASB). Just as a bird alights on its appointed place because it has a right to be there, so a curse alights upon us for a cause. If curses come, there is a reason for them. The reason for curses is clearly stated in Deuteronomy 28.

> "But it shall come about, if you do not obey the LORD your God, to observe to do all His commandments and His statutes with which I charge you today, that all these curses will come upon you and overtake you."
>
> Deuteronomy 28:15, NASB

Once again, the phrase translated, "obey the LORD" is really "listen to the voice of the LORD." So the reason why curses come is twofold: If you will not listen to the voice of the Lord and if you will not do what He says. In other words, curses come for exactly the opposite reason for which blessings come. Blessings come through listening and doing. Curses come through not listening and not doing. That is very logical and very practical.

The Outcome of Disobedience

Let's look briefly now at the curses for disobedience. We have already seen that the basic point of departure from God is not listening to His voice. If we trace the history of clans or tribes or nations that have gone away from God, it always begins there. They cease to listen. Often the beginning is subtle and hard to detect. We can still maintain outward conformity to God's commands for a long while after we have really ceased to listen. But if we trace our problems to their source, they begin when we no longer listen to God.

The full list of curses is very lengthy, a total of 53 verses. Again, you need to read the rest of that chapter for yourself. If you go through the list of curses you will discover that you may be enduring curses when you should be enjoying blessings. That fact alone could perhaps change your whole life and lifestyle.

Here I want to point out some of the main areas covered by the curses.

Mental and Emotional Curses

One main area is mental and emotional, and there are a number of statements made about it.

Verse 20: "The LORD himself will send on you curses, confusion, and frustration in everything you do" (NLT). The two curses there are confusion and frustration. Everything you try to do turns out wrong.

Verse 28: "The LORD will afflict you with madness . . . and confusion of mind" (NIV). Also, verse 34: "The sights you see will drive you mad" (NIV). To be driven mad is a curse. Confusion is a curse.

Verse 65: "The LORD will give you an anxious mind, eyes weary with longing, and a despairing heart" (NIV). The curses there are anxiety, weariness and despair. You see so many people in almost any major city, walking around, bowed down under those curses and not really knowing why the curses have come.

Physical Curses

Now we will move on to the area of the physical, and again the list is long and totally comprehensive.

Verse 21: "The LORD will make the pestilence cling to you" (NASB). Notice that pestilence clings; we cannot shake it off.

Verse 22: "The LORD will smite you with consumption and with fever and with inflammation" (NASB). Three curses: consumption, fever, inflammation.

Verse 27: "The LORD will afflict you with the boils of Egypt and with tumors, festering sores and the itch, from which you cannot be cured" (NIV). The curses there are boils, tumors, festering sores and the itch.

Verse 28: "The LORD will afflict you with . . . blindness" (NIV). Blindness is a curse.

Verse 35: "The LORD will afflict your knees and legs with painful boils that cannot be cured, spreading from the soles of your feet to the top of your head" (NIV). Again boils are singled out as a curse.

Verse 59: "The LORD will bring extraordinary plagues on you and your descendants, even severe and lasting plagues, and miserable and chronic sicknesses" (NASB). What a verse! What a terrible picture! All of those are curses—extraordinary plagues, chronic sicknesses.

Verse 60: "[The Lord] will bring back on you all the diseases of Egypt of which you were afraid, and they will cling to you" (NASB). I spent two years of my life in Egypt, and I want to tell you there are few diseases that are not found in Egypt. These diseases comprise an awful list. And all the diseases of Egypt are part of the curse.

And then, as if that were not enough, verse 61 says: "Also every sickness and every plague which, not written in the book of this law, the LORD will bring on you until you are destroyed" (NASB). So it is not only all the sicknesses and plagues that are written in the book of the Law, but all the rest that are not. In other words, every kind of sickness and every kind of plague is part of the curse.

Family Relationships

There are several other areas dealt with as part of the curse. One area is relationships—especially family relationships. Wrong family relationships are part of the curse. For instance, in verse 30: "You shall betroth a wife, but another man will violate her." And verse 32 reads: "Your sons and your daughters shall be given to another people, while your eyes look on and yearn for them continually; but there will be nothing you can do."

Poverty

One curse that applies particularly to our subject is in verse 29: "You will grope at noon, as the blind man gropes in darkness, and you will not prosper in your ways" (NASB). The Bible is consistent with itself. Just as prosperity is a blessing, so not prospering is a curse. This aspect of the curse is described again more fully in verses 47–48: "Because you did not serve the LORD your God with joy and a glad heart, for the abundance of all things" (NASB).

Let us pause here for a moment and take note that this verse states the positive will of God for His people. It is that we serve Him with joyfulness and gladness for the abundance of all things. If, however, through unbelief and disobedience we do not enter into God's positive will, then the negative alternative is set before us in the next verse: "Therefore you shall serve your enemies whom the LORD will send against you, in hunger, in thirst, in nakedness, and in the lack of all things" (NASB).

Look at that list for a moment: hunger, thirst, nakedness and lack of all things. Picture it. No food, no drink, no clothes—nothing. Sum that up in one word: Poverty. In fact, I would say, *absolute poverty*. You can have no greater poverty than that. Which is it—a curse or a blessing? The answer: Absolute poverty is a curse.

There are other curses listed in these verses of Deuteronomy 28. The full listing of categories is:

Humiliation
Mental and physical sickness
Family breakdown
Poverty
Defeat
Oppression
Failure
God's disfavor

In the next chapter, we will examine the way in which Jesus has dealt with these curses on our behalf so that we can be totally liberated from their effects.

5

The Exchange at the Cross

A basic principle that is consistently emphasized throughout Scripture is that obedience to God brings His provision in all areas of our lives. Deuteronomy 28 lists all the blessings that follow obedience to God and, conversely, all the curses that follow disobedience. We saw that prosperity is listed under the blessings, while poverty is listed under the curses.

Each of us needs to face up—humbly and honestly—to this clear revelation of God's Word. We have to acknowledge that at times we have failed to fulfill the conditions for receiving God's blessings; and on the other hand we have done things that exposed us to the curses. As a result, we have actually experienced curses in various areas of our lives.

Deliverance from Curses

But—thank God!—He has provided a way of deliverance from the curses. This takes us to the cross. One of the great basic truths of revelation is that on the cross a divinely ordained exchange took place. Jesus—the sinless, obedient Son of God—took upon Himself all the evil that was due mankind by divine justice because of our rebellion and disobedience. In return we, through faith, are able to receive all the good that was due to the perfect obedience of Jesus. More simply stated, Jesus took all the evil we deserved, so that we might receive all the good He deserved.

Deliverance is provided for us through one means only, and that is the atoning, substitutionary, sacrificial death of Jesus Christ on the cross.

Scripture unfolds many different aspects of this exchange, which were prophesied seven hundred years before it took place. In Isaiah 53, the prophet says, "All we like sheep have gone astray; we have turned, every one, to his own way; and the LORD has laid on Him the iniquity of us all" (verse 6).

I believe, as did all the writers of the New Testament, that the person referred to there is Jesus. "The LORD has laid on Him [Jesus] the iniquity of us all."

The word translated "has laid" means literally "has made to meet together." The word that is translated "iniquity" means "rebelliousness." But it also means "all the evil consequences of rebelliousness." The same word includes both shades of meaning. So, if we put it that way, we see that the Lord made to meet together on Jesus our rebelliousness and all the evil consequences of our rebelliousness.

Our rebelliousness consists in this: that we have all gone astray. We have each of us turned to his own way. This is the basic problem of the human race. It is not that we have all committed certain specific sins like murder or adultery or robbery. But there is one thing that we all have in common: Each of us has turned to his own way. That is rebelliousness. That is the root problem of humanity: rebelliousness toward God—turning away from His way to our way. And that rebelliousness and all its evil consequences the Lord made to meet together upon Jesus on the cross.

There are many, many aspects to those evil consequences. For instance, Jesus was wounded that we might be healed (see Isaiah 53:4–5). He was made sin with our sinfulness that we might

37

be made righteous with His righteousness (see 2 Corinthians 5:21). He was rejected by the Father that we might be accepted by the Father (see Matthew 27:46; Ephesians 1:5–6). He died our death that we might have His life (see Hebrews 2:9; John 3:16). In this chapter we will focus on an aspect of the exchange that relates to one particular curse that comes to us due to our disobedience—in particular, to the curse of poverty.

Jesus Became the Curse

Paul deals with Jesus' substitutionary death specifically in Galatians 3:13–14:

> Christ has redeemed us from the curse of the law, having become a curse for us (for it is written, "Cursed is everyone who hangs on a tree"), that the blessing of Abraham might come upon the Gentiles in Christ Jesus, that we might receive the promise of the Spirit through faith.

Two words are here set in stark contrast to one another: *curse* and *blessing*. On the cross, the curse of the broken law came upon Jesus. He was actually made a curse. The evidence was the very fact that He hung upon the cross (cited from Deuteronomy 21:23). Suspended between heaven and earth, Jesus hung there on the tree that had become a cross—rejected by man and forsaken by God, totally alienated, cut off, alone. We could sum it up in one evil, ugly word: *accursed*.

Jesus became a curse that we might receive the alternative: the blessing. One of the themes of Galatians is that, through faith, we become the children of Abraham. As the children of Abraham, we are entitled to the blessing of Abraham. God blessed Abraham because he obeyed God's voice. That blessing now becomes our inheritance for one main reason: because Jesus bore the curse.

In other words, the blessing of Abraham covers every area of our lives—spiritual, emotional, physical, financial, relational. Everything is included, and that abundance is made available to us through the sacrificial death of Jesus. Jesus became the curse. He hung there, visibly demonstrated as a curse. The curse of the broken law came upon Him that the blessing of obedience might be available to you and to me as we believe, and that is God's way of deliverance from the curse.

The Promise of the Holy Spirit

In this connection Paul emphasizes one particular blessing in Galatians 3:14: "the promise of the Spirit." There is a practical reason for this. The promised blessing of the Holy Spirit is the key to all the other blessings. Once we put our faith in Christ's atoning death on our behalf, we become legally "heirs of God and joint heirs with Christ" (Romans 8:17). We become members of God's family, entitled to all that was promised to our great forefather, Abraham (see Galatians 3:7–9, 29). But the divinely appointed administrator of our inheritance is the Holy Spirit. He alone can bring us into the full, experiential enjoyment of all that has become legally ours through faith in Christ's death. Without His help, we will fare no better than "orphans," incapable of appropriating all that our Father has provided for us (see John 14:16–18).

Acknowledging our dependence, then, upon the Holy Spirit, we may lay claim to our inheritance. What is "the blessing of Abraham" to which Christ has entitled us? A clear and comprehensive answer is found in Genesis 24:1: "The LORD had blessed Abraham in all things." The blessing of Abraham includes all things—whether they are temporal or eternal, spiritual or material. Through the death of Christ on our behalf, every area of our lives can be brought out from under the dark shadow of the curse into the full sunlight of God's blessing.

This is what Jesus said in John 16:13–15:

> "But when He, the Spirit of truth [the Holy Spirit], comes, He will guide you into all the truth; for He will not speak on His

own initiative, but whatever He hears, He will speak; and He will disclose to you what is to come. He will glorify Me, for He will take of Mine and will disclose it to you. All things that the Father has are Mine; therefore I said that He takes of Mine and will disclose it to you."

NASB

Guided into Our Inheritance

So you see, everything in the universe belongs initially to God the Father, and God the Father has bestowed everything on God the Son. Jesus says, "All things that the Father has are Mine." But the Holy Spirit is the administrator of the inheritance of all the wealth of the Godhead.

It is the Holy Spirit who takes the things that belong to Jesus and discloses them unto us. It is the Holy Spirit who leads us into all the truth. It is the Holy Spirit who shows us our inheritance and shows us how to enter in and claim it.

We need to see these two facts side by side. The legal basis for our deliverance from the curse was provided by the substitutionary death of Jesus on the cross. He became a curse that we might receive the blessing. But the practical process of entering into the blessing depends upon our relationship to the Holy Spirit.

The Holy Spirit is the guide. He is the interpreter. He is the administrator. He is the steward of the entire wealth of God's Kingdom. And so, to pass from theory to experience, from theology to having what God intends us to have, we depend on the Holy Spirit.

That is why Paul emphasizes, particularly, that in passing from curse to blessing, we need to receive the promise of the Holy Spirit. The Holy Spirit is the one who can show you your inheritance. He can illuminate the Scriptures. He can show you what is a curse and what is a blessing. He can point out to you the conditions that you have to fulfill and then He can give you the grace, the faith, the wisdom, to meet those conditions. That is God's way of deliverance from the curse.

Exchange for the Poverty Curse

Let's now focus on one particular aspect of the curse that Jesus bore on our behalf—the poverty curse. In the previous chapter, we saw this curse presented in its most absolute form in Deuteronomy 28:48. It was summed up in four parts: hunger, thirst, nakedness and want of all things. And that is exactly what Jesus experienced on the cross.

Some years ago, while I was preaching on the theme of "God's Financial Provision," I received a revelation from the Holy Spirit that went beyond anything in the sermon outline that I had before me. While I still continued to stand before the people and speak to them, I was having an inner, mental vision of Jesus on the cross. I saw Him there in all the stark reality that Scripture indicates.

One by one, the Holy Spirit went over the four aspects of the poverty curse for me and showed me that Jesus totally exhausted the curse in all its aspects. He was hungry—He had not eaten for nearly a day. He was thirsty—one of His last utterances was, "I thirst." He was naked—the soldiers had stripped Him of all His clothing and shared it among themselves. He was in need of all things—He had neither a robe nor a tomb to be buried in. He had nothing. Why? Because in the divine purpose of God, He exhausted the poverty curse on our behalf.

At first I did not realize the full implication of what the Holy Spirit was showing me. Looking back, however, I would have to say that this revelation changed the course of my life. It gave me a basis for my faith for God's abundance. I saw the absolute finality of the exchange. Jesus took the poverty curse that we might receive the blessing of Abraham "in all things"—that we might receive our full inheritance, ministered by the Holy Spirit.

All grace comes only by way of Calvary. All that God offers in grace is on the basis of what Jesus Christ did by His substitutionary sacrifice on the cross. Abundant financial blessing is offered because Jesus was made poor with our poverty. "For ye know the grace of our Lord Jesus Christ, that, though he was rich, yet for your sakes he became poor, that ye through his poverty might be rich" (2 Corinthians 8:9, KJV).

I used to quote that verse "might *become* rich." Then, with my King James Bible open, the Holy Spirit prompted me to look closer: *Take another look. It says "might* be *rich."* There is a difference. We can become rich and then become poor again. But to "be" rich is permanent. Jesus took the evil, which is poverty, that we might have the good, which is riches. Jesus took our poverty that we might have His wealth.

Notice that exchange. It is exactly the same as the exchange on the subject of sin or sickness or any of the other great exchanges that took place at Calvary. Everything evil was laid upon Jesus that everything good might come upon us. Jesus was made a curse that we might receive a blessing and He was made poor. Let's face the truth, friend, as we ask, Why? It was that we might become rich.

If you think that poverty is holy, why are you fighting against such holiness all your life? Just be logical. If you think poverty is a blessing, as some people say, why then aren't you cultivating it? Be consistent: Aim to be poor. Instead, you spend hours every week avoiding poverty. Surely you are not trying to dodge a blessing!

Oh, the foolishness we have endured so long from people trying to pretend that poverty is a blessing! Oh, the harm that has been done to the cause of God! "He became poor, that ye through His poverty might be rich." That does not suit a lot of religious people. But, friend, by the time we finish here, you will either believe it or disbelieve the Bible. That is the only alternative.

Jesus' Descent into Poverty

When did Jesus become poor? As we noted earlier, some people suggest that He lived in poverty all through His earthly ministry, but I cannot accept this as accurate. Remember the distinction between *riches* and *abundance*. Jesus was not "rich" in the sense of having a large bank account or great material possessions. But as we have seen, He certainly had abundance.

He was never worried. He was never perplexed. He was never under pressure. He never panicked. He was calmly and completely in control of every situation. He never doubted that His Father's goodness would supply everything He needed. And the Father never failed Him. That is not poverty. Poverty is being hungry, thirsty, naked and in need of all things!

So when did Jesus become poor? He began to become poor the moment He was identified with our sins. From that moment onward, He went deeper and deeper into poverty until on the cross He represented absolute poverty.

Let's also face the fact that at that point, His poverty was not merely "spiritual." He was physically and materially poor. Therefore, by all the laws of logic, our wealth will not be merely "spiritual" either. Jesus became absolutely poor in the physical, material sense so that we might become rich in the sense of having every physical and material need met—and having something left over for other people.

Let's look at that crucial aspect of abundance in our next chapter.

6

Lifted by Grace

God is not stingy. He doesn't give just enough. He gives enough and more. That is abundance. God's grace provides abundance, overflow.

The revelation that Jesus took poverty so we could receive blessing is supported by many passages of Scripture in both the Old and the New Testaments. Let's look, in particular, at another verse from 2 Corinthians. This verse and the verse quoted in the last chapter are easy to remember, as the chapter and verse are just reversed: 2 Corinthians 8:9 and 2 Corinthians 9:8. Together these two verses present the full deliverance Christ has obtained for us from the poverty curse.

> God is able to make *all* grace *abound* toward you; that ye, *always* having *all* sufficiency in *all* things, may *abound* to every [*all*] good work.
>
> 2 Corinthians 9:8, KJV, emphasis added

That is the King James Version, but I am going to give you the "Prince version," because in the Greek the apostle Paul uses the Greek word for *all* in one form or another five times in one verse. That is fantastic. Let's look at it again.

God is able to make *all* grace abound toward you; that you, *all* ways having *all* sufficiency in *all* things, may abound to *all* good work.

In that verse, there are two *abound*s and five *all*s. Language cannot be more explicit than that. How could anyone possibly use language more clearly to express complete abundance? God makes all grace abound toward us that we in turn may abound to every good work, and there is no exception. Where is there any room for lack, inadequacy or insufficiency in that verse? There is nothing left out. Let me reiterate those words: God is able to make all grace abound toward you so that in all things at all times, having all that you need, you will abound to every good work. That is a wonderful general statement.

The confession of your faith, however, is personal: "Believe in the heart, confess with the mouth." We can personalize it in this way: *"God is able to make all grace abound toward me; that I, always having all sufficiency in all things, may abound to every good work."* That is my statement of faith. I take the general promise of the Word and I particularize it by the confession of my lips.

That is the provision of God. When the poverty curse was taken by Jesus, God's abundance was made available to us.

Grace and Money

This passage is a description of God's grace. Interestingly enough, in both chapter 8 and 9 of 2 Corinthians, which deal with money, the key word is *grace,* occurring seven times in chapter 8 and twice in chapter 9. We are not preaching law, but we are preaching grace in the realm of finance. Everything we receive of grace comes by Jesus Christ. "For the law was given through Moses, but grace and truth came through Jesus Christ" (John 1:17).

Clearly, it is grace that operates in the realm of money. The Scripture says concerning Jesus, "Of His fullness we have all received, and grace for grace" (John 1:16). Jesus was the gracious giver and one of the graces we receive in Jesus Christ is the grace of giving. Every grace that is in Christ is manifested in the believer. So Paul—in speaking about giving—calls it a *grace*. Not *law,* but *grace.* This is what Paul says: "But as you abound in everything—in faith, in speech, in knowledge, in all diligence, and in your love for us—see that you abound in this grace also" (2 Corinthians 8:7).

What is "this grace"? The grace spoken of here is the grace of giving. The Corinthians abounded in spiritual gifts. They had the gifts of utterance, they had the gifts of knowledge, they were very keen and diligent. They loved Paul, but he said, "There is one grace you still must demonstrate: the grace of giving. See that you abound in this grace also."

Immutable Principles of Grace

Few professing Christians really understand the nature of God's grace, however. I have sometimes observed that those who speak the most about grace often understand it the least. We need, therefore, to point out three basic principles that govern the operation of God's grace.

First, *grace can never be earned.* In fact, anything that can be earned is not grace. "And if by grace, then it [what we earn] is no longer of works; otherwise grace is no longer grace" (Romans 11:6). This excludes most religious people from the grace of God, because they think they can earn it.

Second, *there is only one channel of grace.* "The law was given through Moses, but grace and truth came through Jesus Christ" (John 1:17). Any form of grace that comes to us comes solely through Jesus Christ.

Third, *there is only one means by which we can appropriate God's grace—and that is faith.* This is summed up in three successive phrases in Ephesians 2:8–9: "by grace . . . through faith . . . not of works [not earned]."

Appropriating Material Abundance

Few Christians realize that grace applies in the realm of financial and material provision just as much as in any other area of our lives. For example, some Christians contend that in biblical emphasis love is more important than money. But I say that they cannot be separated. The "love chapter" (1 Corinthians 13) contains thirteen verses. The "money chapters" in 2 Corinthians contain 39 verses—three times as many. Some say the New Testament has nothing to say about money, but this proves otherwise.

Also, as we will see more fully in later chapters, there are usually conditions connected to the promises of Scripture. Regarding finances, Scripture warns us specifically against irresponsibility (see Proverbs 10:4); against laziness (see Proverbs 24:30–34); and against dishonesty (see Ephesians 4:28). As long as we are guilty of any of these sins, we have no right to expect God's grace to work in the financial area of our lives. As Christians, we are obligated to be honest, hard-working and responsible.

But all of our hard work and responsibility in itself does not earn us the kind of provision we are talking about here. Such provision cannot be earned. It can be received only by grace through faith. God's grace, when we thus receive it by faith, lifts us onto a higher level than we can ever earn or deserve. This is true in every area of our lives—the financial and material no less than the spiritual.

Recognizing this truth, however, leads us to an important logical distinction—one that is frequently overlooked. It is the distinction between *earning God's grace,* which is impossible, and *meeting God's conditions,* which is obligatory.

On the one hand, we cannot earn God's abundance, which comes only through grace. On the other hand, we must meet the requirements that God has laid down for receiving His abundance through faith. Otherwise, if we do not meet the requirements, our faith has no scriptural foundation. In fact, it is not faith, but mere presumption.

We turn then to the requirements that Scripture sets before us—certain principles to understand, steps to follow and conditions to be met if we are going to receive God's full provision for our lives. In the next three parts of this book, we will observe these principles, steps and conditions.

PART 2

FIVE PRINCIPLES
OF PROVISION

7

Where Your Provision
Comes From

Now that we have laid the groundwork for understanding abundance, we will explore the five basic principles regarding God's provision, one in each of the next five chapters. Each of these principles is solidly based upon the promises of Scripture.

Do you have a need? Is there a promise in God's Word that fits your situation? The first principle teaches us that in order to live within and then share from God's abundant supply, we need to believe His promises as stated in Scripture.

Principle 1: All of God's promises hold our provision.

All the basic principles of God's abundance are related in some way to His promises. We see this most clearly from 2 Peter 1:2: "Grace and peace be multiplied to you in [*through*, KJV] the knowledge of God and of Jesus our Lord."

Note that the Christian life is a life of multiplication. It is not static—just a matter of holding on to what you have. It is not even mere addition. It is *multiplication*. This comes through "the knowledge of God and of Jesus our Lord." Everything that we ever need comes to us from God, the source, through Jesus, the channel. No other channel or source of supply is needed:

as His divine power *has given* to us all things that pertain to life
and godliness, through the knowledge of Him who called us by
glory and virtue, by which have been given to us exceedingly
great and precious promises, that through these you may be
partakers of the divine nature, having escaped the corruption
that is in the world through lust.

verses 3–4, emphasis added

Notice the tense that Peter uses: God *has already given* us all
we are ever going to need—for time and eternity, for every area
of our lives—pertaining to life and godliness. Many times we
pray on the basis of a misunderstanding, asking God to give
us something He has already given us. It is not easy for God to
answer those prayers because, by answering them, He would
support the misunderstanding. Sometimes we have to adjust our
thinking in order to pray the kind of prayer that God is able to
answer. *Thanking* God is often more appropriate than *petition-
ing* Him, for God has already given us everything.

Notice again, all is included in the knowledge of Jesus Christ.
The Greek says, "Jesus called us to *His own* glory and virtue"
(verse 3, emphasis added). This is not our glory, but His. It is
not our virtue, but His. God has already given us everything we
are ever going to need, and it is all contained in the knowledge
of Jesus.

The Greek word for *knowledge* can also be translated "acknowledging." It means both "knowledge" and "acknowledging." It is not enough that we intellectually *know about* Jesus;
we must effectively *acknowledge* Him in our lives.

The next words of that passage hold the key: "By which
have been given to us exceedingly great and precious promises."
God has *already* given us everything we are ever going to need.
Where is it? It is *in the promises of His Word*. God's *provision*
is in His *promises*. This is the vital truth that you must grasp.

Say this statement over and over to yourself until it becomes
part of your thinking: *All of God's promises hold our provision.*
If you do not know the promises in Scripture, if you do not

relate to the promises, then you do not receive the provision. It isn't because God has not made the provision, but because you have not discovered or are not willing to avail yourself of it.

Partakers of God's Nature

Now we come to another breathtaking statement in 2 Peter 1: "That through these [the promises] you may be partakers of the divine nature" (verse 4).

I often wonder if the human mind can understand or absorb that language. It means that we become *partakers of God's own nature*. If I had not read it in the Bible I am not sure that I could accept it. But it is there clearly in the Bible. Through the promises of God, you and I, as believers—redeemed by the blood of Jesus, coming to God the Father through Jesus Christ the Son—become partakers of God's own nature. We receive the very nature of God within ourselves.

Now, you may think that is a risky statement to make. And it is! Yet Scripture supports it. When Jesus was challenged about His claim to be the Son of God, He quoted one of the psalms, saying, "If He called them gods, to whom the word of God came (and the Scripture cannot be broken)" (John 10:35). The quotation is taken from Psalm 82:6, which says, "I said, 'You are gods.'" God actually spoke to humans and said, "You are gods."

We may find this hard to receive, but Jesus gives us the divine commentary. How could humans become gods? What was the basis? It was that the Word of God came to them: "If He called them gods, *to whom the word of God came* (and the Scripture cannot be broken). . . ." The same principle applies to us.

Because the Word of God comes to us through the promises of God, we can become partakers of God's nature. We can become divine. I realize, of course, that statement could be misused; nevertheless, I believe that, in the way I have presented it, it is an accurate analysis of what Scripture actually teaches.

Escaping Corruption

And then the next statement is also breathtaking, but it is a very logical consequence. The final part of that revelation in 2 Peter 1 is: "Having escaped the corruption that is in the world through lust" (verse 4). In proportion as we become partakers of the divine nature, we escape the corruption that is in this world caused by evil desires—spiritual, moral, even physical corruption. That is because the divine nature and corruption are incompatible. The divine nature is incorruptible; everything in this world is corruptible. As we receive the promises of God, they impart to us the nature of God, and as we receive the nature of God, we are delivered from the corruption that is in the world through lust. All this comes through the great and precious promises of God's Word.

I would like to sum up in my own words the essence of what Peter has told us in verses 3–4 above, reduced to five successive statements:

- God's divine power has already given us everything we are ever going to need for time and eternity.
- God's provision is all contained in rightly knowing and acknowledging Jesus.
- All of God's provision is in His promises.
- As we appropriate the promises, we become partakers of God's nature.
- As we become partakers of God's nature, we are delivered from the corruption of this world.

I suggest that you should not merely read through this five-point summary once—or even twice. Take time to meditate on it. The revelation is such that you cannot absorb it in just a few readings. It demands that you expose your whole mind and being to it until it becomes a part of you.

8

Stepping into Your Inheritance

There is a very simple parallel between the Old Testament and the New. In the Old Testament, under a leader named Joshua, God brought His people into a Promised Land. In the New Testament, under a leader named Jesus (which in Hebrew is the same name as Joshua), God brings His people into a land of promises.

Old Covenant—a Promised Land.

New Covenant—a land of promises.

This brings us to our next principle regarding God's abundance:

Principle 2: All of God's promises are our inheritance.

Our inheritance is what God is bringing us into. Yet even though He has given it to us, we still have to lay claim to it.

A Legal Transaction

I want to illustrate this from the historical example of the Israelites entering into their inheritance, the land of Canaan. Moses brought Israel out of Egypt and into the wilderness, but Moses could not bring them into the Promised Land. God raised up another leader, Joshua, and commissioned him, after the death of Moses, to bring Israel into the Promised Land.

Let's look for a moment at Scripture and see the basic conditions God gave to Joshua. First God said, "Moses My servant is dead" (Joshua 1:2). I find this very significant. Before we can come into something new, there always has to be a death of something old. The spiritual life, in a certain sense, is like the seasons of the year. There is a continuing, ongoing cycle of seasons. There is summer with its abundance; then fall, a time of withering; winter, the time of death; and then spring, the time of renewal and resurrection. This is a principle that goes through our lives. God only blesses that which has died and been resurrected.

The transition from Moses to Joshua represents one that recurs from time to time in the life of every believer.

> "Moses My servant is dead. Now therefore, arise, go over this Jordan, you and all this people, to the land which I am giving to them—the children of Israel. Every place that the sole of your foot will tread upon I have given you, as I said to Moses."
>
> Joshua 1:2–3

Again, it is important to notice the tense of the verbs. In the first verse God says, "I am giving the land" to Israel. In the very next verse He says, "I have given it to you," in the past tense. It is important to see that as soon as God gave the land, the land had been given. Nothing had changed physically; they were still in the same position. The visible ownership of the land had not changed in the least bit. But because Almighty God said, "I am giving you the land," from that moment onward, legally, the land was theirs. It *had been given* to them. Just as we saw in the first principle—the promises hold the provision—God has *already given* us everything. How? By giving us His promises as our inheritance.

Stepping into the Promises

The way in which Joshua and Israel entered into their inheritance is a pattern for us. First of all, they had to understand that the land from then on was legally theirs. Second, they had to do something about it.

What did they have to do? The Lord said to Joshua, "Every place on which the sole of your foot treads, I have given it to you." So, they had to go in on the basis of what God had told them, believing that the land was legally theirs. And they had to assert their ownership by placing their feet on the land that God had promised. God said to them, "As soon as you put your foot on any piece of soil in the land, it is yours—legally. It is yours already, but to make it experientially yours, to have it in actual experience, you have to go in and put your foot on it."

That is exactly how it is with us as Christians. We have to do just as Israel did. First of all, we have to believe what God has said—that legally it belongs to us because God has given it to us. Second, we have to act. We have to move in and, as it were, place our feet on every area that God has promised. As soon as we experientially place our feet on that area in faith, it becomes ours in reality. Israel entering the Promised Land is a pattern for us who are entering the land of promises.

Recently I noticed something in Joshua 1:2 that I had never seen before. The Holy Spirit emphasized the word *all*—"all this people." God was not going to leave any of the people behind. In most circles today, we would be satisfied if we could get 90 percent of the people over. But God said, "Everyone is going to go over." I really believe that is how God views our situations today in regard to His promises.

Everybody who wants to receive will have to move in—"You and all this people." Sometimes when I have talked with believers about being baptized in the Holy Spirit or receiving some further provision of God, they reply, "I got it all when I was saved. There's nothing more to get."

My answer to that is usually: "If you got it all, where is it all?"

Nevertheless, I do believe in a sense that their statement is correct. Legally, when you come to Christ, you become an heir of God and joint-heir with Jesus Christ. Thereafter, the whole inheritance is legally yours. But there is a great deal of difference between the legal and the experiential. You may own much legally, but enjoy very little in actual experience.

I sometimes illustrate this by the following little parable: If Joshua and the children of Israel had been like some Fundamentalists, they would have lined up on the east bank of the river Jordan, looked across the river, folded their arms and said, "We've got it all!" That would have been legally correct, but experientially incorrect. If they had been like some Pentecostals, they would have crossed the river Jordan—which I liken to being baptized in the Holy Spirit—then lined up on the west bank, folded their arms and said, "We've got it all!" But, actually, though they would have been one stage further, they would still have been far from their real inheritance.

Laying Claim to Our Promise

The interesting fact about the children of Israel taking the Promised Land is that God brought them in by a miracle, and then gave them their first victory over Jericho by a miracle. But after that, they had to fight for every piece of land they possessed. You and I must not expect to get our inheritance without conflict either!

The way they were to gain their inheritance was this: "Every place that you put the sole of your foot upon shall be yours." So it is with us also.

Legally, it is all ours right at the moment of conversion. Experientially, however, we have to move in and assert our claim to that which God has given us. We have to put our foot on each promise as we come to it. This is a very vivid picture for our assertion: "God has promised this to me, and I now lay claim to His promise."

9

Expressions of God's Will

Suppose a father says to his young son, "Son, I want you to clean the garage. If you'll sweep it out and put everything in order, make it nice and clean and do a good job, I'll give you ten dollars." So the boy goes off and works for a couple of hours, sweeps out the garage, does a good job, makes everything beautiful and orderly.

He then comes back hot and perspiring and says, "Dad, I've done just what you asked. I want you to come in and see the garage. It's really nice and clean." The father walks in, inspects the garage, and says, "Yes, it's nice. It's good." And the son says, "Dad, can I have my ten dollars?" The father says, "Oh, I never intended to give you the ten dollars."

How would you evaluate a father like that? He would not have your confidence, nor could he have his son's confidence.

What I want to tell you is, God is not a father like that. God does *not* say, "If you do this, I'll give you ten dollars," then when you have done it, turn around and say, "Well, I never meant to give you ten dollars." In other words, whatever God promises to do, that is His will to do.

If we discover a promise that meets our need, and we obediently fulfill the conditions that God has laid down, then we have understood and applied the first two principles.

If we then come to Him for what He has promised, He will never tell us, "It's true that I promised you that, but I never really meant to give it to you. It's not My will." Such behavior would be unbecoming even in an earthly father. It would be totally inconsistent with the nature of God as our heavenly Father. God is not inconsistent. He is not whimsical. He is not illogical.

In fact, Jesus Himself has assured us that the very opposite is true: "If you then, being evil, know how to give good gifts to your children, how much more will your heavenly Father give the Holy Spirit to those who ask Him!" (Luke 11:13). We see, then, the third principle of God's abundant provision for His people:

Principle 3: All of God's promises are the expression of His will.

God never promised anything that was not His will. It is very important that we understand that this is how it is with the promises of God.

Coming in Faith

God did not have to make the promises. They are all the expression of His grace. He could have given us no promises at all. But in making His promises available to us in His Word, He made Himself available. He revealed to us His will. And so, when you come to God on the basis of His clearly stated promises, and you know you have understood them in the way they were intended—when you come to God on that basis, then you know it is the will of God. You can pray in faith knowing the will of God and knowing that when you pray He hears you and you have what you prayed for.

You see, in most cases where our faith is being tested or where we are seeking answers to prayer, the vital issue is the will of God. When we know God's will, we can pray with confidence. This is expressed in 1 John 5:14–15.

> Now this is the confidence that we have in Him [God], that if we ask anything according to His will, He hears us. And if we know that He hears us, whatever we ask, we know that we have the petitions that we have asked of Him.

Please notice, the issue is the will of God. If we know that we are praying according to God's will, then we know that He hears us. And if we know that He hears us, then we know that we have what we asked of Him. It is granted. That does not mean we have it immediately in experience, but we know it is settled. The provision is there for us.

So the vital truth in prayer, and in the whole life of faith really, is knowing the will of God. God has graciously revealed His will to us in His promises. That is how we know the will of God. If God promises to do something, it is His will to do it.

The Greek word translated "confidence" in 1 John 5:14 (quoted above) means literally "freedom of speech." It was a very important word in the political background of the Greek people. One of the rights they fought for in democracy was freedom of speech, which is, of course, very dear to democratic nations. So that verse could read: "This freedom of speech we have in God." The implication is that confidence needs to be expressed in what we say. It is not enough merely to believe "with the heart"; we must also confess "with the mouth" (see Romans 10:10).

Successful Praying

All successful praying revolves around the knowledge of God's will. Once we know that we are asking for something according to the will of God, we know we have it. Not "we're going to have it," but "we have it."

Let's take a moment to consider some Scriptures that support this concept of receiving what we pray for. The first passage is Matthew 7:7–8, which is taken from the Sermon on the Mount. In six different ways, it states that God wants you to get what you pray for.

> "Ask, and it will be given to you; seek, and you will find; knock, and it will be opened to you. For everyone who asks receives, and he who seeks finds, and to him who knocks it will be opened."

Please notice that there is not one negative suggestion in all those words. In six different ways, Jesus tells us that God wants us to pray and to get what we pray for.

In Matthew 21:22, Jesus says: "All things, whatsoever ye shall ask in prayer, believing, ye shall receive" (KJV).

How could it be any clearer than that? All things, whatsoever ye shall ask, ye shall receive.

In John 14:13–14, Jesus says: "And whatever you ask [the Father] in My name, that I will do, that the Father may be glorified in the Son. If you ask anything in My name, I will do it."

What could be more emphatic or more all-embracing than that statement? If you shall ask anything in His name, He will do it.

In John 15:7, we read: "If you abide in Me, and My words abide in you, you will ask what you desire, and it shall be done for you."

And John 16:24 says: "Until now you have asked nothing in My name. Ask, and you will receive, that your joy may be full."

Jesus challenges us to ask and to receive the answer so that our joy may be full. Experience convinces me (and I believe most have found it true as well) that there is nothing that gives fullness of joy more wonderfully than knowing that Almighty God answers your prayers. What could be more wonderful than to know that the Creator of the universe, the One who has all power, is attentive to the voice of our prayer and delights to do that which we ask? When we find that in experience—to pray and receive a specific answer to our prayer—our joy is full. That is why Jesus said, "To have fullness of joy, ask, and you will receive."

Of course, there are basic principles and conditions for regularly receiving the answer to your prayers. Later in this book, we will deal systematically with the main conditions for getting your prayer answered. As we go through those conditions later, I want you to bear in mind this great, basic fact we are stating here: God wants you to pray and to get what you pray for. Do not let the conditions become a fence that keep you from praying. Certainly, we have to observe the conditions. But the great basic realization we need is that God really wants us to pray and He really wants us to get what we pray for.

Finally, we see in Mark 11:24 that Jesus says: "Therefore I say unto you, What things soever ye desire, when ye pray, believe that ye receive them" (KJV). The correct, literal translation of *receive* is actually "received." When do we receive? *When we pray.* The verse concludes: "And ye shall have them" (KJV). The receiving is in the present. The actual, experiential outworking of what we have received—the "will have them"—is often in the future. But if we do not receive *now,* we will not have *then.*

The teaching of Mark 11:24 agrees exactly with that of 1 John 5:14–15. In each case, the lesson is: We must receive, by faith, *at the very moment that we pray.* Thereafter, we must boldly express our confidence that we have received—even before that which is received is actually manifested in our experience.

This takes us to our next principle.

10

The Promises Are for Now

I want to emphasize three very short, but very important, words in this next principle. The three short words are: *all, now* and *us*. Keep those words in mind as you read.

Principle 4: All of God's promises are now available to us through Christ.

One of the devil's favorite tactics is to get us to put off to some future moment that which we ought to appropriate now. In my book *Faith to Live By* (Whitaker House, 1977), I illustrate this tactic with a story that has always been vivid to me. As a young man of about twenty, while I was studying Greek philosophy at Cambridge University, I received a grant to visit Greece in order to study the various antiquities that were located there. I went with a friend of mine who was the son of the vice-chancellor of Cambridge University. We stayed in a hotel in Athens, and went out about the same time every morning for the day's sightseeing.

Every day when we walked out of our hotel, there was a little group of shoeshine boys on the sidewalk waiting to polish our shoes. If you have never been to the Mediterranean countries, you will find it hard to picture the scene, but in those countries these children are determined! I mean, they are going to polish your shoes whether you want it or not! Every morning these boys would approach us and say, "Shine your shoes?" Every morning we would say in Greek, "No!"—"*Ochi!*" When you say no in Greek, you say *ochi* and you throw your head back at the same time. The motion of the head enforces the meaning of the word. But every morning these shoeshine boys simply went ahead and polished our shoes anyhow.

Since our method of refusal was not working, one morning my friend decided to try a different tactic. When we got out of the hotel door, the shoeshine boys approached us asking, "Polish your shoes?" This day my friend replied in Greek, "*Avrio.*" His reply caught the boys off guard. They paused for a moment and looked at us uncertainly. Taking advantage of their momentary hesitation, we got by without having our shoes polished.

Can you guess what *avrio* means? It means "tomorrow."

Many times when you are on your way to appropriating God's blessings, the devil resorts to the same tactic. He does not say no; he says, "Tomorrow." As a result, you hesitate just for a moment and so fail to appropriate the blessing you are praying for.

What does Scripture say is the accepted time? Now! People often say, "*Today* is the accepted time." But Scripture does not say that. It says, "*Now* is the accepted time . . . *now* is the day of salvation" (2 Corinthians 6:2, emphasis added).

God lives in the eternal now. When you meet God, it is never yesterday and never tomorrow. His name is not "I was" nor "I will be." It is always "I AM." (See Exodus 3:14.)

Yes and Amen

As a basis for this principle of appropriating God's promises *now*, let us look at 2 Corinthians 1:20. This is a key verse when addressing the topic of dispensationalism—which is a concept that relegates nearly all of God's blessings and provisions either to the past ("the apostolic age") or to the future ("the millennium").

This particular verse is not easy to translate into English. There are a number of different ways to translate it, but they all amount to the same thought in the end. Here I am going to quote two translations—first of all the New International Version, then the King James.

> For no matter how many promises God has made, they are "Yes" in Christ. And so through him the "Amen" is spoken by us to the glory of God.
>
> NIV

> For all the promises of God in him [Jesus Christ] are yea, and in him Amen, unto the glory of God by us.
>
> KJV

Consider the NIV first. It says, "No matter how many promises God has made, they are all 'Yes' in Christ." In other words, for every promise God has made, if we come to Him in the name of Jesus and claim it, then God says yes.

The NIV continues, "So through him the 'Amen' is spoken by us to the glory of God." When God says yes, then we respond with amen, and that settles it. Our responding with amen is like our putting our feet on that particular area of ground. This applies to every promise you can find in the Bible. If you come to God on the basis of that promise, through Jesus Christ, God says yes. And when God says yes, you say amen to that promise—and that settles it.

It seems to me that the King James Version says it about as clearly and emphatically as it is possible to say it, and is easier to explain. "For all the promises of God in him [Jesus] are yea, and in him Amen, unto the glory of God by us."

If an alternative translation is still needed, I would suggest, "God gave all the promises to be yes, and He fulfilled all the promises to be Amen in Jesus." But whatever translation we follow, there are certain key words that do not change.

First of all, it is *all the promises*—not some, but all. All the promises of God—every promise God has ever made, is yes in Christ.

Second, it says *are*—not "were" or "will be." All the promises of God are in the now. So many people believe God did wonderful things in the past. They believe He will do wonderful things in the future. But just at the moment, they view God as being kind of bankrupt. His promises are in abeyance. But that is not what the Bible says. The Bible says all the promises of God now are yes and amen.

Third, the promises are *in Him,* Jesus. There is only one channel through which God makes His promises available to us. That unique, all-sufficient channel is Jesus. Abundance comes to us only from the source, God, through the channel, Jesus. Outside of Jesus we have no claim on God's promises for provision.

Fourth, they are given *to the glory of God.* Every promise that we appropriate in the will of God glorifies God. The ultimate purpose of God's abundance is God's glory. God has so arranged His promises that when we appropriate them, He is glorified. And so, in claiming the promises of God, we bring glory to God.

Finally, there are two little words that come last in 2 Corinthians 1:20 (KJV): *by us.* It is not "by the apostles" or "by the early Church" or "by special Christians," such as evangelists or missionaries or pastors. It is "by us." And *us* means you and me. All God's promises are now available to you and me through faith in Christ.

The Glory Due Him

Romans 3:23 says, "All have sinned and fall short of the glory of God." There are different ways of translating that verse, but in essence I understand it to mean, "By our sin we have robbed

God of His glory." How, then, do we repay to God the glory due Him? Well, Romans 4 says about Abraham that:

> He did not waver through unbelief regarding the promise of God, but was strengthened in his faith and gave glory to God, being fully persuaded that God had power to do what he had promised.
>
> Romans 4:20–21, NIV

Notice how Abraham gave glory to God. It was on the basis of God's promise. God's promise is the basis on which we can give Him glory. By believing His promises, we give back to God the glory that our sin has robbed from Him. That is the very essence of sin—that we have robbed God of His glory. The more we claim God's promises, the more we glorify Him. And all His promises are now available to us through Christ.

Of course, you do not need all of God's promises right now. In fact, you could not claim all of God's promises in just one moment. But any promise you need that fits your situation is available to you right now.

This is the way I sum it up: Every promise that fits our situation and meets our need is for us now.

11

Focusing on the Promise

This last principle is where so many people miss out. They find the promises. They set out to claim their inheritance. They find something tremendous and wonderful that God has promised and they are all excited and enthusiastic. Then they look at their situation and the circumstances they are facing, and they apply the brakes. They say, "Well, God couldn't meet this need. My situation is too difficult. Of course, God really intends to do it. But in my particular situation, it just wouldn't be possible."

That is one big mistake that we make continually. Instead of focusing on the promises, we turn away, look at the situation and miss out on the promises. We need to grasp this principle:

Principle 5: All of God's promises being fulfilled does not depend upon our circumstances but upon His power.

When God gives a promise, it is not limited to a particular set of circumstances. It does not have to be easy for God to do what He promised to do. The truth of the matter is, God's promises do *not* depend upon the circumstances in which we find ourselves. Circumstances make no difference. You can be a man who is a hundred years old with a wife who is ninety years old, but if God says you are going to have a son, you are going to have a son.

Let me make a bold statement here: We do not need to try to make things easy for God. God wants to work in such a way that the glory goes only to Him. Remember: The purpose of God's promises that pour forth His abundance is His glory. In a certain sense, the more impossible it is, the more the glory goes to God.

It does not depend on anything around you or in you. Nothing physical or temporal—nothing in the time/space world can change the eternal promises of God. That is the lesson, and it is why God so often allowed biblical men and women of faith to get into totally impossible situations. He wanted to make it absolutely clear that in no case were His promises dependent upon a favorable set of circumstances. In fact, He usually let the circumstances become just about as unfavorable as they could be.

Elijah, Israel and Gideon

Real faith refuses to be influenced by circumstances. Look at these three instances.

When Elijah wanted the fire to come down from heaven to consume the sacrifice on his altar, he doused the sacrifice in water three times. He let the water run around and fill up the ditch. Then he said, "Now let's see what God can do." And when the fire came, it burned up the water, it burned up the dust, it burned up the wood and it burned up the sacrifice. God's fire has no more problem with a ditch full of water than with dry wood. Wet or dry, difficult or easy, possible or impossible—it makes no difference with God. (See 1 Kings 18:20–40 for the full story.)

When Israel crossed the Jordan into the Promised Land—and you will remember that this is a pattern for us—the Jordan was in flood stage. It was at its highest point. It flowed the fastest of any time of the year. God did not want it to be easy. He chose a time when it was most difficult.

Now think of God's dealings with Gideon. Gideon started out with 32,000 men to fight the Midianites. God said, "You have too many men; let some of them go. If they're afraid, let them go home, because if you win the battle with 32,000 men, people will say Israel did it by their own power." So Gideon released those who were afraid and let them go home. The first group who left were 10,000, which left 22,000. God said, "There are still too many. Take them down to the brook and let them drink. The ones who lap the water, putting their hand to their mouth, are the ones you can take." Only 300 men met that condition. From 32,000, God whittled the army down to 300 because He wanted the glory for Himself. He wanted to exclude the possibility that Israel had done it without God.

Everything Is Ready

There are two Scriptures that have become very real to me in this context, both from Luke 22. The first is:

> And He [Jesus] said to them [the disciples], "Behold, when you have entered the city, a man will meet you carrying a pitcher of water; follow him into the house which he enters. Then you shall say to the master of the house, 'The Teacher says to you, "Where is the guest room where I may eat the Passover with My disciples?"' Then he will show you a large, furnished upper room; there make ready."
>
> Luke 22:10–12

This is so typical of the Lord's dealings as we follow His directions. When we get to the place He is leading us to, everything has already been made ready.

You might wonder how the disciples could recognize the particular person carrying a pitcher of water. Well, Jesus said it was a man. In the Middle East it is very common to see women carrying pitchers of water, but rare to see a man do this. So this was a distinctive sign. When they obeyed the directions and followed the man, they came to the place.

This is a picture of how God deals within our lives. We must find His leading, and we have to follow, but when we get to where He is taking us, everything has already been made ready. That has been God's pattern in my life—and yours, too, whether you recognize it or not. That is just how He deals with us.

We read earlier the verse in which Jesus, speaking to His disciples again, said: "'When I sent you without money bag, knapsack, and sandals, did you lack anything?' So they said, 'Nothing'" (Luke 22:35).

You may ask, Why did He send them out without money bag, knapsack and sandals if He knew they were going to need them? The answer is because the Lord always wants to keep us continually dependent on Him for the things we need.

If you study God's dealings with Israel, He continually dealt with them that way. For instance, when He brought them out of Egypt and they were following His supernatural sign all the way, He brought them to a place where the Red Sea was in front of them and the Egyptian army behind them. God brought them there. They had not made a mistake. God got them there because that was where He wanted them—in a place where they needed Him desperately and no one else could help them.

After that, they marched out into the desert on the other side of the Red Sea and they followed the Lord three days. They had no more water, and they came to this wonderful pool of water called Marah. But when they tried to drink it, it was too bitter. They could not drink it. God had led them all that way. It was not that they had made a wrong turn and come to the wrong place. Why did God bring them there? Because He wanted them to know that they were totally dependent on Him.

There was only one person among them who was clever enough to recognize that. They all murmured and complained, but Moses prayed and God showed him what to do to make the water sweet.

Wilderness Provision

Perhaps the most remarkable example of this principle, that the provision of God does not depend on our circumstances, is God's care for Israel in the wilderness. For forty years, God fed, clothed and guided something like three million people—men, women, old people, infants, plus their cattle, everything. This was in a totally barren desert where there was no water, no food—nothing, in fact, except sand and sun. God went out of His way to assert, "Let Me show you what I can do." *He* made it difficult. He was the one who arranged the situation.

What follows is an excerpt from *Streams in the Desert* by Mrs. Charles Cowman (Zondervan, 1965) on this tremendous act of God, caring for three million people in the wilderness for forty years.

It is not the great achievement of the Red Sea crossing by Moses and the Israelites that is so stupendous and miraculous. The awesomeness of the Wilderness Journey is the fact that approximately three million people were sustained for forty years in a small, dry, fruitless desert. Have you thought of what it must have been like to merely exist from day to day with every human means for survival out of reach? Let us look at a few facts to see how impossible it would have been for Moses and his people to rely upon their own means of subsistence: "To get through the Red Sea in one night they had to have a space at least three miles wide, so they could walk 5,000 abreast. If they walked double file, it would have been 800 miles long, and it would have taken them 35 days and nights to get through. . . . The amount of food for consumption alone is absolutely astounding when you consider the fact that they were traveling in a country where there was no abundance of natural food to be found. Just the amount needed to keep from starving would have added up to 1,500 tons a day. . . . Then consider the amount of water required for barest necessities of drinking and washing dishes each day. It has been calculated that they would have to have 11 million gallons every single day."

Now consider those figures and bear in mind that those numbers were not for the whole forty years. They were for every single day of the forty years. In other words, God placed His people by His own decision and plan in a situation where every natural source of supply was not available. He did that to let them know that He is Almighty, that He keeps His promises, that He can be relied on, and that He is not limited to any particular set of circumstances or any particular situation. What was true for Israel is true for you and me.

It is most important to understand that you must not let your focus move from the promise to the situation. Whenever you do that, like Peter walking on the water, you will begin to sink.

The Principles Are in Place

Let's review the five basic principles of God's provision. Understanding these principles gives us a solid foundation for taking the next step.

Principle 1: All of God's promises hold the provision. If we fail to claim God's promises, we cannot expect to receive His provision.

Principle 2: All of God's promises are our inheritance. In the Old Testament it was a Promised Land. In the New Testament it is a land of promises.

Principle 3: All of God's promises are the expression of His will. When we appropriate God's promises, we pray with confidence because we know we are praying according to God's will.

Principle 4: All of God's promises are now available to us through Christ. Every promise that fits our situation and meets our need is for us now.

Principle 5: All of God's promises being fulfilled does not depend upon our circumstances, but rather upon our meeting God's conditions. The outstanding example of this is

Israel's forty years in the wilderness when God provided for some three million people without any natural resources whatsoever.

These principles assure us that God's promises are in place. In Part 3 we discover three simple, practical steps for appropriating every promise that meets our every need.

THREE PRACTICAL
STEPS TO TAKE

12

How to Appropriate
God's Promises

As we open our hearts and minds to the revelation of God's desire to bless us with abundance, and as we stand on the scriptural principles He has laid out for us, we become ready to receive the promises with gratitude.

It is here that we turn to the administrator of our inheritance for guidance. As with many aspects of God's promises, it is incumbent upon the believer to be sensitive to the direction of the Holy Spirit in appropriating what God has made abundantly available. Sometimes there is a timing issue. Sometimes there is a character issue God wants to deal with. So while we can move confidently into the provision God has promised in a general sense, that does not remove our obligation to hear from God in a specific sense in each situation we encounter. It is so important to follow the prompting of the Holy Spirit, avoiding presumption and any hint of a sense of entitlement. With that in mind, here are three steps for appropriating God's promises of abundance.

Step One: Let Him Pick the Promise

First, let the Holy Spirit direct you to the appropriate promises.
This is very important. It really is not up to you to select the
promise you want. I am familiar, of course, with the idea of
keeping a "Promise Box," a small box filled with promises of
Scripture written on cards, and handing it to people to let them
select one. Many times in my experience, God actually did work
through that practice—but only if it was led by the Holy Spirit.

The Holy Spirit is the one who shows us the promise that is in
the will of God and relevant to our situation at any given time.
When the Holy Spirit directs us to a promise, He also imparts
to us the faith to appropriate that promise. In the last resort,
the initiative is with God and not with us. We make no demands
on God. We give no orders to God. But by being sensitive to the
Holy Spirit, we discover God's will for us in any given situation
revealed in His promises.

I have had need of healing from God several times in my
Christian experience. It is interesting to me as I look back how
the Holy Spirit would direct me to a particular Scripture promise
for a particular situation. If I tried to take hold of that same
Scripture promise in the next situation, however, it did not work
because that was not where the Holy Spirit was directing me.

Seeing the Holy Spirit As a Person

You just cannot reduce God to a formula. God is Spirit. You
cannot put the Spirit in a box or reduce the Spirit to a math-
ematical equation—that is not how it works. But if you relate to
the Holy Spirit as a Person, make friends with Him and become
intimate with Him, He will direct you into your inheritance in
the promises.

Here is what Jesus says about the ministry of the Holy Spirit—
and notice that He did not call the Holy Spirit "it." He called
Him "He." He is a Person. This is very important to our understanding of our inheritance. Jesus said:

"But when he, the Spirit of truth, comes, he will guide you into all truth. He will not speak on his own; he will speak only what he hears, and he will tell you what is yet to come. He will bring glory to me by taking from what is mine and making it known to you. All that belongs to the Father is mine. That is why I said the Spirit will take from what is mine and make it known to you."

John 16:13–15, NIV

On that basis, the Holy Spirit is the administrator of the total inheritance. All that belongs to the Father belongs to Jesus. But what belongs to the Father and to Jesus is administered or imparted to us by the Holy Spirit. He takes what belongs to Jesus and makes it known to us. As we receive from the Holy Spirit, we really become heirs to the whole inheritance.

Following His Ongoing Leading

The initiative is with the Holy Spirit. He is the one who guides us into all truth. If we part company with the Holy Spirit, we will soon find that we have parted company with the truth. We are not capable of coming into the real truth of God apart from the guidance of the Holy Spirit. The Holy Spirit in any given situation, knowing God's plan for our lives and knowing the Word of God perfectly, will direct us to that part of the Word of God that will also fulfill God's plan for our lives.

Another Scripture says very briefly the same thing: "For all who are being led by the Spirit of God, these are sons of God" (Romans 8:14, NASB).

That concept is in the continuous present tense: Those who are continually being led by the Spirit of God, they are the children of God. This is not a once-for-all contact, but an ongoing association with the Holy Spirit. As we are regularly and continually led by the Holy Spirit, we live as sons of God. We become children of God through the new birth—through being born again of the Spirit. But we live as God's mature sons and daughters when we are regularly led by the Holy Spirit.

81

Step Two: Examine the Conditions

The second step to appropriating God's promises is this: *When the Holy Spirit has led you to a given promise in the Word of God, study and fulfill the conditions.* You see, most of God's promises are conditional. In most cases, the promises of God begin with a word like *if.* God says, "If you do this, I will do that." It is childish and immature to try to claim God's promise without studying and fulfilling the condition. You cannot ignore the *if.* You cannot try to tie God down to doing something He has promised to do on certain conditions if you do not first meet the conditions.

A very good example of this is a promise very close to me.

If thou wilt diligently hearken to the voice of the LORD thy God, and wilt do that which is right in his sight, and wilt give ear to his commandments, and keep all his statutes, I will put none of these diseases upon thee, which I have brought upon the Egyptians: for I am the LORD that healeth thee.

Exodus 15:26, KJV

This is a tremendous promise! God says, "I will put no sickness upon you. I'll be your healer." But you cannot claim that without noting the *if.* There are four conditions:

If you will diligently hearken to His voice.
If you will do that which is right in His sight.
If you will give ear to His commandments.
If you will keep all His statutes.

On the basis of those four conditions, God says, "I am the LORD that healeth thee." Do not claim the Lord as your healer and bypass the conditions. We will talk more in Part 4 about conditions that we must meet.

There are, of course, some unconditional promises of God. Acts 2:17 is one example: "And it shall come to pass in the last days, says God, that I will pour out of My Spirit on all flesh." I understand this to be an unconditional promise of God related to a certain time. Likewise, I believe that God's promise of the restoration of Israel at the same period is unconditional. So there are some promises where God says, "I will do this unconditionally when it suits Me." Most of God's promises, however, are conditional and we need to learn what the conditions are.

Step Three: Believe and Act

The third step to appropriating God's promises is this: *Maintain an attitude of faith and act appropriately.* There is both attitude and action. You must adopt a posture of believing and then, where appropriate, you must act in accordance with what you believe. Scripture says, "Faith without works [that is, appropriate acts] is dead" (James 2:26).

Let me give you two Scriptures from Hebrews that emphasize this. The first is: "That you will not be sluggish, but imitators of those who through faith and patience inherit the promises" (Hebrews 6:12, NASB).

Notice, it is not enough to have faith. You must have faith and patience. When you have located the promise, and when you have met the conditions, you have to hold on in an attitude of faith or trust until the promise is fulfilled. There is often a period of time between your meeting the conditions and the promise being fulfilled. That is the test of whether you really have faith.

The second verse is: "For you have need of endurance, so that when you have done the will of God, you may receive what was promised" (Hebrews 10:36, NASB). The same principle is true here. There is a time lag. You do the will of God, you meet the conditions, and then you hold on. Do not give up. In due course, in God's sovereignty, the promise is completely fulfilled. It is very important to maintain that attitude of faith and to act accordingly.

Let me give you a brief example that comes to my mind. Some years back a woman who had been crippled in childhood with infantile paralysis came to be healed at a meeting where I was ministering. One of her legs was about one and a half inches shorter than the other, and she wore a shoe with a corresponding build-up. When I ministered to her, by the grace of God, the short leg moved down a full one and a half inches and she stood up on equal legs for the first time in many years. Then she opened a brown paper bag she had with her to pull out a new pair of shoes with no build-up. She had brought them with her because she was certain that she would walk away with her legs equal.

I said to myself, *That's a good example of faith and works.* She had maintained the attitude of faith and she had acted according to what she was believing. So she did not have to go out after the meeting and look for a pair of shoes without a build-up. She already had them with her. It was one of the greatest and most inspiring acts I have ever seen from a child of God.

A Scripture Promise Example

Let's take an example and see how these three steps might be taken. Then in the next chapter, we will use this as a model for any individual promise that you receive for a particular need.

Suppose the Holy Spirit has impressed you with the two Scriptures that follow. When you read these verses they seem to leap off the page at you. Perhaps your minister spoke on these verses and you knew in your heart that God was directing them toward you.

> Oh, fear the LORD, you His saints! There is no want to those who fear Him. The young lions lack and suffer hunger; but those who seek the LORD shall not lack any good thing.
>
> Psalm 34:9–10

For the LORD God is a sun and shield; the LORD will give grace and glory; no good thing will He withhold from those who walk uprightly.

Psalm 84:11

Whatever way you received them, you knew that the Holy Spirit spoke to you, and you thus took the first step in appropriating this aspect of God's provision: *You let Him pick the promise.*

Notice the clear statement at the end of Psalm 34:10, "Those who seek the LORD shall not lack any good thing." Again, at the end of Psalm 84:11, "No good thing will He withhold from those who walk uprightly." Both are clear promises that God will provide everything good that you need.

Before you plunge into claiming these very beautiful promises, however, you need to take the logical second step: *Now you examine the conditions.* Neglecting this step is where many people go astray. They say. "Oh, that's a beautiful promise. I want that." But they don't pause to examine the conditions. As we said earlier, most of God's promises are conditional. He says, in effect, "If you do *this*, I will do *that*."

You need, then, to do some simple biblical analysis. You need to discover the conditions that are attached to the promises, bearing in mind that the promises are given only to those who fulfill the conditions. Combining the two passages, we find that there are altogether three simple conditions clearly stated in these verses. Can you pick them out?

The first condition is *fear the Lord;* the second, *seek the Lord;* and the third, *walk uprightly.* Provided you meet these three conditions, Scripture says God will withhold no good thing from you. Isn't that exciting?

Let me go back over the promises and show you where the conditions come. Psalm 34:9 says: "Oh, fear the LORD, you His saints! There is no want to those who fear Him." It does no good simply to say there is no want if you miss out on the fact that this promise applies only to those who fear the Lord.

Psalm 34:10 says: "The young lions lack and suffer hunger; but those who seek the LORD shall not lack any good thing." Now, it is childish just to say, "Isn't that wonderful! I am not going to lack any good thing!" We cannot omit the condition, which is, "seek the Lord." The promise is only for those who seek the Lord.

Then, in Psalm 84:11, the latter part of the verse says; "No good thing will He withhold from those who walk uprightly." Again, it is childish to say, "I've just discovered that the Lord won't withhold any good thing from me!" You cannot say that. But you *can* say, "I've just discovered that if I walk uprightly, the Lord will not withhold any good thing from me."

Any preacher who tells you that you will not want for any good thing without qualifying that statement or impressing upon you the conditions that God has laid down in His Word is really not doing you any service. Such a misguided belief will cause you to start out with the impression that everything is going to be fine. Then you will find out, after a little while, everything is far from fine. But do not blame God. You may perhaps blame the preacher, but you must really accept the responsibility yourself. You tried to claim the promise without examining and fulfilling the conditions.

As you meet the conditions, you then take the third step: *You maintain an attitude of faith that God is working to fulfill this promise for you.* You might thank Him that He is bringing the desired result to you. You might, like the woman with the uneven legs, prepare for the answer. You hold on in an attitude of trust, waiting patiently.

The promise of these particular verses is stated in similar language in both passages. In Psalm 34:10 it says, "Those who seek the LORD shall not lack any good thing." In Psalm 84:11 it says, "No good thing will [God] withhold from those who walk uprightly." The bottom line of the promise is this: You shall not be in want of any good thing.

That is a wonderful promise, and one that God delights to fulfill for His people in many different ways promised through many different Scriptures to meet many different circumstances.

When Questions Remain

God's provision is ready. The Holy Spirit guides us into the promises. Further, we can be assured that when we follow these steps, we will receive the answer according to God's will.

Why then, when we look around us, do we see so many people continue in their need? If they have received God's Word on the subject, have endeavored to meet the conditions, and have done their best to act in faith, why does it seem as though it just doesn't work for them?

Generally, the answer lies in a misperception of what is good. In other words, there are two ways in which a thing may be good. Many Christians do not understand this, and consequently they are frustrated, and they think that something has gone wrong or that the promise they thought they received is not really for them.

We need to do some further analysis in the realm of logic.

13

Is Your Desire Good?

We are continuing to explore a promise from Psalms 34 and 84—not lacking any good thing. While this is a specific example from Scripture to use as a model for taking the three steps to fulfillment, it is also pertinent to our topic of the promise of abundance. Many times, Christians feel that they are being greedy or vain to seek a promise of abundance. Can we really expect—even pray—not to lack any good thing?

The key word in these promises is *good*. No *good* thing will God withhold from those who meet His conditions. Before we decide that something we desire is good, however, we need to ask ourselves two further questions.

First, is the thing good in itself? To use philosophic terminology, is the thing *absolutely* good? This is the invariable in a situation. Something that is absolutely good is always good.

Second, we need to ask: Is the thing good for us in our particular situation? To use philosophic terminology once again, is the thing *relatively* good? This is the variable in each situation. Something that is good in itself may not be good for us in our particular need. In other words, it may be absolutely good but not relatively good.

For This Time and Place?

This distinction has a very direct and practical bearing on how God deals with us. All of us discover, sooner or later, that there are times when we ask God for something that we are convinced is good, and yet God withholds it from us. In other words, God does not automatically hand out that which is absolutely good each time we ask for it. Rather, He first determines whether the thing is relatively good. Is it good for us in our particular situation? Sometimes God withholds from us that which is absolutely good because it is not relatively good. That is, it is not good for us in our particular situation at that particular time.

Let's say, for example, that a businessman has discovered a new invention. He believes he will make a tremendous fortune, but he lacks the capital to get it launched. He is a Christian, so he prays saying, "God, if I had a hundred thousand dollars, I could get this thing launched. I'd make millions and I'd give nine-tenths of my income to You." It all sounds very good. God, who is a very smart businessman, happens to know that it really is not a viable invention and is not going to make millions of dollars.

The hundred thousand dollars the man prayed for is, in itself, essentially good. But, for that man in that situation, it is not relatively good, because if he gets the hundred thousand dollars, he will enter into a tremendous commitment, set up a factory and end up bankrupt. So God, in His wisdom and in His mercy, withholds the hundred thousand dollars. Again, this is not because the money is not essentially good, but because it is not relatively good for that man in his particular situation and his particular condition.

Take another example. A wealthy man has a teenage son. The teenage son has an ambition to own one of the latest, most powerful and most expensive sports cars. The father is perfectly able to buy his son the car, but he knows that his son's character is not fully developed. He is unstable and emotional. He wants to impress all his friends and if he gets that car, it is more than probable he will end up in a wreck. The father can easily afford ten cars like that. Nevertheless, when his son asks for the car for his sixteenth birthday, the father says no.

That expensive sports car, in the terminology we are using, is essentially absolutely good. It is beautifully manufactured and well put together—it is very smart and attractive. It is essentially good. But for that son, at his age with his emotional instability, it is not relatively good. If it is put into his hands, without his exhibiting self-discipline, training and maturity, it will be an instrument of destruction and not of good.

Those are crude examples, but they serve to illustrate how God deals with us. At times we find ourselves in situations where we ask God for something that is good but we don't receive it. God is not saying, "It isn't good." He is saying instead, "It's not good for you just now in the light of your character, your situation, your weaknesses, your problems, your misunderstandings." God may withhold that which is absolutely good when it is not relatively good.

Looking back over a walk with the Lord that has lasted several decades, I thank God for the many prayers of mine that He has answered. But I also thank God with all my heart for some of the prayers He did not answer. When I see where I could have been if God had answered some of my prayers, I say, "Thank You, God, that You were wise enough not to give me what I asked for."

When we see that truth, it solves many of our problems of unanswered prayer. We realize that our prayers did not really go unanswered. God just answered in a different way from what we expected. Sometimes we forget that even no is an answer.

How to Evaluate Wealth

Bearing in mind the distinction we have established between that which is absolutely good and that which is relatively good, let us now examine the group of concepts we outlined earlier that have to do with provision: riches, wealth, prosperity, abundance. How does Scripture evaluate them? Are they, in themselves, bad? Or are they good—*absolutely* good?

We are not discussing now whether they might not be relatively good in a certain situation, but we are focusing on them in their essential, absolute nature. Are they absolutely good? We are not going to go to human wisdom or religious organizations or libraries for our answer, but we are going to the Word of God.

What does the Word of God have to say about it? It answers clearly: Yes. All these things are essentially good. Many of us have grown up with the impression that somehow wealth is wicked. It is sort of the same attitude that was instilled into us as children about the medicines we were required to take. I, for one, was told that the worse they taste, the more good they do for you!

When the Lord saved me and baptized me in the Holy Spirit, I went through a tremendous personal struggle to break away from the concept that insisted, in essence, "If you are going to be a Christian, prepare to be miserable." Many years later, I heard Pat Boone give a similar testimony. He said that as a young boy growing up, and then in high school, he came to the conclusion that if he were to become a committed Christian it would mean seventy years of misery and then heaven at the end—and he wasn't sure that heaven would be worth seventy years of misery!

The questions I want to pose are: "Is poverty good or bad? Are riches good or bad?" Rather than having our answer based on emotional response or religious tradition, I want one that is logical, objective and scriptural. The answer will have a decisive effect on the way we follow the three steps for appropriating God's promises to their conclusion.

If riches are bad, we should dissociate ourselves from them. We should not in any way be involved in any of the activities or processes that would generate wealth. It is my conviction, however, that Scripture clearly and consistently gives the opposite answer: *Riches and wealth are essentially absolutely good.* There are multitudes of Scriptures that we could look at to support this conclusion, but I must content myself with providing just a few.

In Good Company

The first verse is Revelation 5:11–12. In this passage the angels and the living creatures and all the hosts of heaven are speaking. They are voicing the unanimous consensus of all heaven. Their evaluation is absolute and unchanging.

> Then I looked, and I heard the voice of many angels around the throne, the living creatures, and the elders; and the number of them was ten thousand times ten thousand, and thousands of thousands, saying with a loud voice: "Worthy is the Lamb [the Lamb of God, the Lord Jesus Christ] who was slain to receive power and riches [or wealth] and wisdom, and strength and honor and glory and blessing [or praise]!"

My conviction is that every one of those seven items in verse 12 is essentially good, and they all belong by eternal right to the Lord Jesus Christ. The second one mentioned there is riches or wealth. Let's look at the others: power, wisdom, strength, honor, glory and blessing. That puts riches in very good company, doesn't it? All these seven items are essentially absolutely good.

On the other hand, all—or nearly all—of them can be misused and abused. Obviously, power can be misused and abused, and very often is. Likewise, strength is good, but there are many people who abuse it to bully, to harm others, to impose their will unjustly and unrighteously. That does not mean that strength is not good. It means that something good can be abused.

The same is true of wisdom. Wisdom is essentially good and yet there are people who use wisdom for their own ungodly ends—to cheat, to deceive and to get things for themselves that they are not entitled to. That does not mean wisdom is not good. Solomon is an example of a man who had tremendous wisdom and misused it, for he ended up in idolatry.

The fact that something is absolutely good in itself does not mean that it cannot be abused or misused. But we would be very foolish to refuse something simply because it can be abused. And yet, this is one of Satan's favorite tactics—to make us refuse something good because we have seen it abused.

I worked in East Africa for five years with a Pentecostal missionary organization based in Canada. After about a year, I realized that they practically never exercised any gifts of the Spirit. So I asked. "Why don't we have any gifts of the Spirit in operation?"

They responded, "Oh, in Canada they've been misused."

But that is not logical! So what if they have been misused? Does that mean we are not to use them? If that is sufficient reason for not availing ourselves of God's provision, then there will be nothing good left to us, because the devil can always find people to misuse any good thing.

Yet multitudes of Christians are influenced by this kind of reasoning to the point where they no longer appropriate what is good and what is theirs by right because somebody has misused it. For my part, I cannot accept such reasoning. No matter if the whole world misuses riches! If it is good, I want it! Likewise wisdom or power or strength or honor or glory or blessing.

The Ultimate Source

One important factor in evaluating if something is good or bad is to determine its source. For our second passage of Scripture, we turn to 1 Chronicles 29. This is part of a prayer of worship and dedication that David prayed to the Lord at the time he was preparing for the building of the Temple. What he says here are some of the most glorious words in the Bible.

> Yours, O LORD, is the greatness and the power and the glory and the majesty and the splendor, for everything in heaven and earth is yours. Yours, O LORD, is the kingdom; you are exalted

as head over all. Wealth and honor come from you; you are the ruler of all things. In your hands are strength and power to exalt and give strength to all.

1 Chronicles 29:11–12, NIV

Many beautiful and glorious attributes are ascribed there to the Lord: greatness, power, glory, majesty, splendor. And then again, strength and power. But in the middle of that beautiful prayer, David says to the Lord, "Wealth and honor come from you." Wealth and honor are two excellent things that come from God.

God is the ultimate source of wealth and honor. Anything that originates from God must be good in itself.

You may think that I am overemphasizing, but I can assure you that if you come from a certain kind of religious background, one of the greatest struggles you are going to have is to accept the fact that abundance is essentially good. It is not wicked. It is not sinful.

There are many other passages in Chronicles to confirm that truth, but we will not take time to look at them. Rather, we will look at a third parallel text in Deuteronomy where Moses speaks to Israel. He says that the Lord is going to bring them into an abundant and plentiful land. When they get in there and have all that abundance, they must be careful not to forget where the abundance came from. That is a really important lesson. This is what Moses says:

"But remember the LORD your God, for it is he who gives you the ability to produce wealth, and so confirms his covenant, which he swore to your forefathers, as it is today."

Deuteronomy 8:18, NIV

Who gives us the ability to produce wealth? God. Many individuals misuse that power, but it comes from God. Why does God give it to His people? "To confirm [*establish*, NKJV] His covenant." It is part of God's covenant commitment to His people.

94

Let us therefore focus on the covenant-keeping faithfulness of God, rather than on the unfaithfulness of men who often misuse the power God gives them.

When I found this Scripture, I understood that the ability to produce wealth is a gift from God. God gives it to His people, not because we deserve it, but because it is part of His covenant. In His covenant He promised all blessings, all good things, to those who would make and keep a covenant with Him. And so, in His eternal faithfulness, even though we may not be as wise and deserving as we ought to be, God gives the ability to produce wealth that He may confirm His covenant. This is part of His covenant commitment.

The Unlikely Millionaire

There was a man in Britain some years ago whose interview appeared in the newspaper. Years previously, he had applied for a job as a janitor, though he could not read or write. They said, "You're very suitable. Just sign your name on this application form."

He said, "I can't sign my name. I don't know how to write."

So they said, "Then we can't give you the job."

Having been turned down as a janitor, he started to sell cigars. The result was that he became a millionaire. The man interviewing him said, "Isn't that remarkable? You can't even sign your own name and you've become a millionaire. Why, just think what you would be if you could sign your name."

To that the man replied, "I'd be a janitor!"

If you think about the wealthy people you know, you will find that wealth is not necessarily a result of education. The most unlikely people get rich. Doubtless there are some overall principles that apply. Nevertheless, the ability to gain wealth is not to be explained purely in natural terms. Ultimately, its source is God.

Abundance, then—whether riches or honor or strength—is essentially good. It is part of the provision God has planned for

His people. It is a blessing that flows into your need—as you let the Holy Spirit guide you, as you study and fulfill all that He requires, and as you stay faithful in attitude and action. These three steps lead to the blessing of abundance.

These steps, as we have outlined them, involve a specific Scripture promise for a particular need. There are also general conditions that, once understood, can help us walk in a life of abundance. Part 4 outlines those five conditions.

FIVE CONDITIONS FOR
GOD'S ABUNDANCE

14

Admitting Your True Motive

The purpose of God's abundance is this: for every good work. This means that abundance is not for our own selfish end. It is not for our own satisfaction or glorification. But it is for every good work.

We will take a look at various kinds of good works for which God makes His abundance available a little later. Here I want to deal specifically with the conditions for receiving God's abundance. I would suggest that there are five main conditions presented in Scripture. In short, these are:

1. Our motives and attitudes must be right.
2. Faith is essential.
3. Giving is a scriptural way to show honor.
4. We must think, speak and act rightly.
5. We let God add in His own way and time.

In this chapter we will be taking a closer look at the first of these conditions: *Our motives and attitudes must be right.* In the next four chapters, we will examine the remaining four conditions.

God Looks at the Heart

It is very easy to look to God for His abundance but to have wrong motives and wrong attitudes. Motives and attitudes are of primary importance with God. God does not look at us as we look at ourselves or even as we look at one another. In the book of 1 Samuel the Lord told Samuel something very significant when he came to anoint one of the sons of Jesse to be the future king of Israel. Samuel looked at the first son, who was tall and handsome and impressive, and he thought, *This must be the Lord's anointed*. But the Lord spoke to him and told him something that is of general significance and consequence in all our relationships.

> The LORD said to Samuel, "Do not consider his appearance or his height, for I have rejected him. The LORD does not look at the things man looks at. Man looks at the outward appearance, but the LORD looks at the heart."
>
> 1 Samuel 16:7, NIV

That is the very essence of what we are talking about. God does not see as we humans see. We just look at the outward appearance—we hear the words, we see the appearance and we form our conclusions. But the Lord looks below the surface—at a person's motives and his or her heart attitude.

Might you be looking toward God's provision with a heart attitude that does not honor Him? I want to suggest two main safeguards that will help you handle abundance in a wise manner. The first is: Check your motives. The second is: Check your attitude toward the poor.

Check Your Motives

Why are you seeking abundance in a particular area? Is it out of personal ambition? Is it out of covetousness? Is it out of pride?

Are you self-centered or are you really sincerely seeking the extension of God's Kingdom? Check your motives.

This principle of selfishness can apply, for instance, in the realm of business. Two individuals may be in the same kind of business, pursuing the same goals, using the same methods. Outwardly there is nothing to distinguish the one from the other. But inwardly the motives of one are selfish, whereas the other is genuinely concerned with extending God's Kingdom. So God will withhold abundance from the former—the one whose motives are selfish—but will grant abundance to the latter—the one who sincerely desires to extend God's Kingdom. There is nothing on the surface that would indicate why God would do that. But God looks below the surface. He looks at the motives and the attitudes of our hearts.

In Luke 12 Jesus tells the parable of the rich man who built bigger barns and filled them with his produce. But the Lord said to him, "Fool! This night your soul will be required of you" (verse 20). Jesus then adds this comment: "So is he who lays up treasure for himself, and is not rich toward God" (verse 21). The first direction in which we need to be rich is toward God.

Friend, I wonder how it is with you. If God were to say to you, "Your soul will be required from you tonight," would God also have to call you a fool because you have been rich for yourself, but not rich toward God? It is important to ask how we can protect ourselves against wrong motives, which can be so deceptive and yet so disastrous.

In 1 Timothy, Paul gives a very solemn warning about our motives, and this is especially sobering for Christians:

> People who want to get rich fall into temptation and a trap and into many foolish and harmful desires that plunge men into ruin and destruction. For the love of money is a root of all kinds of evil. Some people, eager for money, have wandered from the faith and pierced themselves with many griefs.
>
> 1 Timothy 6:9–10, NIV

Alas, I have seen that happen to believers whom I have known. Eager for money, they wandered from the faith. Their motives changed. They began to put money before God and before the Kingdom of God. They pierced themselves through with many griefs.

Do not have an ambition to get rich. Have instead an ambition to serve God and to extend His Kingdom.

Self-Examination Regarding Wealth

We would all do well to examine our motives very carefully, because we can so easily fall into temptation when we consider abundance—particularly in the area of wealth. What are some of the ways we go wrong? Here are four areas.

It Is Wrong to Make Wealth Our God

In Colossians 3:5, Paul says that covetousness is idolatry. In other words, when we become greedy—grasping for money—we are making money our god. That is idolatry.

Also, in 1 Timothy 6:10 Paul says, "The love of money is a root of all kinds of evil." The King James says, "The love of money is *the* root of all evil," but that is somewhat overstated. What the Greek actually says is, "The love of money is *a* root of all evil." So out of that evil love of money—that covetousness—all other forms of evil can spring forth in our lives.

It Is Wrong to Seek Wealth by Unethical Means

There are many Scriptures on this subject, but we will look at Proverbs 28:8: "One who increases his possessions [or wealth] by usury and extortion gathers it for him who will pity the poor."

A man may procure a lot of money for himself by crooked means. But ultimately it will be taken from him and given to someone who will pity the poor. There are laws that govern the utilization of money just as certainly as there are laws that govern the cultivation of the crops we plant in the earth.

Jeremiah 17:11 points to the same lesson: "As a partridge that hatches eggs which it has not laid, so is he who makes a fortune, but unjustly; in the midst of his days it will forsake him, and in the end he will be a fool" (NASB).

Again, we are dealing with a law that works as universally as the law of gravity. I can look back and think of men—dishonest, rapacious men—in whose lives I saw this law work out to its disastrous conclusion.

It Is Wrong to Trust in Wealth

Proverbs 11:28 says, "He who trusts in his riches will fall." In my lifetime I have seen that exact result happen to many people who trusted in riches. Likewise, Jeremiah 9:23–24 tells us not to trust in wealth:

> "Let not the wise man glory in his wisdom, let not the mighty man glory in his might, nor let the rich man glory in his riches; but let him who glories glory in this, that he understands and knows Me, that I am the LORD, exercising lovingkindness, judgment, and righteousness in the earth."

We must be careful, then, not to boast or glory in wisdom, strength or riches. They may all be good things, but none of them must be that in which we glory.

It Is Wrong to Use Wealth Selfishly

There are some generous people who are always giving away and always getting richer. Conversely, there are some stingy people who never give and yet get poorer. It is always wrong to use wealth selfishly. Proverbs 11:24 says, "There is one who scatters, yet increases more; and there is one who withholds more than is right, but it leads to poverty."

Proverbs 23:4–5 says, "Do not wear yourself out to get rich; have the wisdom to show restraint. Cast but a glance at riches, and they are gone, for they will surely sprout wings and fly off to the sky like an eagle" (NIV). That describes a person who looks at riches with a wrong motive, one who is selfish and ambitious.

Check Your Attitude Toward the Poor

As you check your motives regarding abundance, particularly in the realm of riches, look also at your attitude toward the poor. This is an area in which we must pay careful attention (and this is related to not being selfish).

There are many different kinds of Christians in the world today with different backgrounds. Some Christians come from backgrounds where they were actually trained to have an attitude of care and compassion for the poor. I am not a Catholic myself by background, but I would like to say that in many areas of the Roman Catholic Church there is a real strong godly emphasis on caring for the poor and the needy. On the other hand, in some sections of what is known as the Evangelical church, there is such an emphasis on being saved by faith that sometimes good works have almost dropped out. Many evangelicals are in danger of ignoring the clear teaching of Scripture that we have an obligation to the poor.

I am going to cite a number of passages of Scripture that bring out clearly the obligation that all of us have to be charitable and compassionate and to offer practical help to the poor, as well as the serious consequences for despising or exploiting the poor. A number of these passages are taken from the book of Proverbs. Put together, they are very powerful in their impact.

Don't Shut Your Ears

Proverbs 21:13 says, "If a man shuts his ears to the cry of the poor, he too will cry out and not be answered" (NIV).

God says that if you shut your ears and fail to answer when you hear a poor person cry to you for help, the time will come in your life when you will be crying out for help, but you will not get an answer. This is a serious warning for all of us. We might say to ourselves, "Well, I'm not in need. I'm not crying out." But there is none of us—without the mercy and grace of God—who can ever be absolutely sure we never will be in need. God says there may come a time when you will be in need, crying out for help. In the meanwhile, if you have answered the cry of the poor for help, then you have the assurance that your cry will be heard and answered.

Choose Righteousness

Proverbs 29:7 says, "The righteous considers the cause of the poor, but the wicked does not understand such knowledge."

There is a clear dividing line between the righteous and the wicked. One scriptural mark of righteousness is to consider the cause of the poor, and one evidence of wickedness is not to understand such knowledge. If we are careless, casual or selfish in our attitude to the poor, the Bible describes that as wickedness.

Lend to the Lord

Proverbs 14:21 says, "He who despises his neighbor sins; but he who has mercy on the poor, happy is he." Proverbs 19:17 says, "He who has pity on the poor lends to the LORD, and He will pay back what he has given."

When we display right motives by being gracious to the poor, then we are not only giving to the poor but also lending to the Lord. And I can tell you, it is a good policy to lend to the Lord. Speaking out of personal experience extending over more than forty years, I know that when you give to the poor and lend to the Lord, there will come a time in your life when the Lord will pay back what you loaned. And the Lord gives a good rate of interest on loans! In a certain sense, it is just enlightened self-interest to be good to the poor.

Avoid Curses

Proverbs 28:27 tells us, "He who gives to the poor will not lack, but he who hides his eyes will have many curses."

This is a guarantee from God in His Word. If you give to the poor, you will never want. But if you shut your eyes to the needs of the poor, there will be many curses that will come upon you.

Follow the Gospel

The New Testament likewise emphasizes consideration for the poor as an essential part of Christian righteousness. In Galatians 2:1–10 Paul describes the confrontation he and his coworkers had with James, Peter and John concerning the way in which the Gospel was to be presented to the Gentiles. The tension was eventually resolved by each group acknowledging the distinctive calling of the other. But there was one point on which both groups were unanimous—to "remember the poor" (Galatians 2:10). We see, then, that remembering the poor and needy is an essential part of the Gospel message.

Today it is easy for some of us to shut our hearts to the needs of the poor. They are not right in our pathway. They are not right before our eyes. They are in another land or nation. They are in the Third World or the inner city, or just "somewhere else." If we are not even aware of the fact that there are poor who need help, we are guilty—because the knowledge is available to us.

These Scriptures—and many others like them—place a tremendous responsibility upon us not to be indifferent but to have concern for the needs of the poor. We simply must not avert our eyes from their plight.

The One Who Fears the Lord

Psalm 112 paints a picture of the one "who fears the LORD" and of the blessings he enjoys. It is worthwhile to study this picture in detail. For the moment, however, let me just point out some aspects that relate to our present theme. (Note also that in 2 Corinthians 9:9, Paul quotes verse 9 of this Psalm, applying it specifically to us as Christians.)

> Wealth and riches are in his house, and his righteousness endures forever. . . . It is well with the man who is gracious and lends . . . for he will never be shaken; the righteous will be remembered forever. . . . He has given freely to the poor, his righteousness endures forever.
>
> Psalm 112:3, 5–6, 9, NASB

In this picture of the God-fearing individual we see three elements woven together:

unshakable righteousness
wealth
generosity to the poor

I am deeply impressed, too, by the counsel Daniel gave to King Nebuchadnezzar. Daniel was one of the court counselors to King Nebuchadnezzar of Babylon. Nebuchadnezzar had a dream he was very troubled about, which predicted some kind of judgment that was to come upon him. He summoned Daniel for the interpretation of the dream. Daniel was very concerned because he saw this as a clear prediction of judgment upon the king. But then Daniel offered King Nebuchadnezzar this advice:

> "Therefore, O king, let my advice be acceptable to you; break off your sins by being righteous, and your iniquities by showing mercy to the poor. Perhaps there may be a lengthening of your prosperity."
>
> Daniel 4:27

What was the specific, practical way in which Nebuchadnezzar could demonstrate that he had truly repented and turned from wickedness to righteousness? By showing mercy to the poor! Had Nebuchadnezzar done that, who knows whether he might have been spared the judgment of God?

As we conclude our examination of the first condition for receiving God's abundance—that which relates to our motives and attitudes—it will be helpful to review the principles we have gleaned.

First, we must guard against following the wrong motives: in particular, making wealth our god, seeking wealth by unethical means, trusting in wealth or using wealth selfishly.

Second, in our attitude to the poor we have seen that it is wrong to despise or oppress the poor or to be indifferent to their need. On the contrary, Scripture requires us to show mercy to the poor in active and practical ways.

Now let us turn to the second condition for receiving God's provision.

15

Faith Is Essential

The second condition for receiving God's provision is essential—it is *faith*. We have already seen that abundance is a part of the provision made for us by the grace of God. Like every provision of grace, it can be received only by faith. We can never overemphasize the importance of faith. It is the primary, indispensable requirement for leading the Christian life.

Faith as the essential condition is brought out in many places in the New Testament, but we will look at just a few of those passages. First of all in Hebrews:

> But without faith it is impossible to please Him [God], for he who comes to God must believe that He is [*exists,* NIV], and that He is a rewarder of those who diligently seek Him.
>
> Hebrews 11:6

Notice that there is a *must* in that verse. Anyone who comes to God *must*—this is an unvarying requirement of God. Must do what? Must believe. That is, must exercise faith. He must believe two things: first, that God exists. I think most people believe that, but that by itself is not enough. He must also believe that God rewards those who earnestly seek Him.

Many people who come to God are not really convinced that if they earnestly seek God, He will reward them. But Scripture says that is the basis on which we must come to God—that if we earnestly seek Him, we believe He will reward us, He will meet our needs, He will fulfill His promises.

That is the basic requirement: We must believe. We must believe that if we seek God earnestly, He will reward us.

Then in Romans we have one of the great key verses of the New Testament: "In it [the Gospel] the righteousness of God is revealed from faith to faith; as it is written, 'But the righteous man shall live by [his] faith'" (Romans 1:17, NASB).

In that key verse, the word *faith* occurs three times. The righteousness of God is revealed from faith to faith and the revelation is this: The righteous one shall live by his faith. The only basis for righteous living that is acceptable with God is the faith basis. We must live by faith.

The word *live* is one of the most all-inclusive words that we can use. It covers everything we do, simple or complicated, regular or unusual. It covers such things as eating, sleeping, talking, walking. It covers every activity. All those activities must be based on faith if we are to be reckoned righteous with God.

A little later on in Romans, Paul sums up the opposite side. In dealing with the question of eating, he says: "But he who doubts is condemned if he eats, because he does not eat from faith; for whatever is not from faith is sin" (Romans 14:23).

Notice that latter part—everything that does not come from faith is sin. Put the two together: *The righteous one shall live by his faith* (the only basis of righteous living is faith) and *everything that does not come from faith is sin*. Paul says it both ways, positive and negative, and living includes everything. Paul applies it to eating, but it applies just as much to our finances.

As we study the area of provision, we need to realize that one of the areas in which God will reward our earnestly seeking Him, if we meet the conditions, is in the area of finance. Many Christians do not exercise faith in the area of finance. Consequently, they are not operating on the only acceptable basis of righteousness. You may be just an ordinary wage earner. You may think you have no special opportunities to exercise faith, but the truth of the matter is that you too must exercise faith for your finances. Do not limit God to doing just what your salary would seem to indicate as possible. You must live by faith in the area of finance.

Our finance has to be based on faith for us to be reckoned righteous before God in that area of our lives. When we handle our money in an unbelieving way, it will lead to results that are sinful: avarice, stinginess and even withholding from God that which is His due. The entire matter of how we dispose of our money must be based on faith.

Giving Comes First

Let's now consider how we can apply the principle of faith in the matter of finance. In the gospel of Luke, Jesus makes it very clear.

> "Give, and it will be given to you. A good measure, pressed down, shaken together and running over, will be poured into your lap. For with the measure you use, it will be measured to you."
>
> Luke 6:38, NIV

Faith acts in obedience to God's Word without waiting to see the promised reward. Give first, and it will be given to you. When we act in faith, we give first. That act of first giving before you receive is faith. Jesus says, "Don't wait to receive. Start to give." When you give, it will be given back to you far more abundantly than you gave. But the measure in which you gave ultimately determines the measure in which you will receive. Receiving follows in God's time. The increase will be based on the measure in which you gave.

Jesus said: "It is more blessed to give than to receive" (Acts 20:35). As long as you are only on the receiving end, you have only the lesser blessing. God so loves His children that He wants all of us to have the greater blessing. He wants us to be in a position where we do not merely receive, but we can be in a position to give. That is one main reason why He promises His abundance to us—so that we can enter into the greater blessing of not just receiving but giving. It is more blessed to give than to receive. This is not just a nice pious sentiment. If you put it into practice, you will find that it is a blessing to receive, but it really is a much greater blessing to give. That is why God makes abundance available to us—because He does not want any of us to be deprived of the blessing of giving.

There are various specific ways in which the Bible directs us to give. The Bible does not leave us to speculate or decide for ourselves how we are to give. Rather it provides us with certain objectives, certain directions into which we should channel our giving.

If we wait until we can "afford it," we are not giving in faith. When we see this truth from the perspective of faith, we can never be too poor to give. On the contrary, part of the remedy for poverty is to begin giving in faith. When the widow gave her last two mites to the Lord, Jesus praised her for it. He did not rebuke her for being "extravagant" or "unrealistic." (See Luke 21:1–4.)

Farming Principles for Finances

Paul implies that the same kind of laws that operate in agriculture also apply in the financial realm. If we want to reap, first of all we have to sow. Speaking to Christians about the way they should give their money to the work and to the people of the Lord, Paul says:

> But this I say: He who sows sparingly will also reap sparingly, and he who sows bountifully will also reap bountifully. So let each one give as he purposes in his heart, not grudgingly or of necessity; for God loves a cheerful giver.
>
> 2 Corinthians 9:6–7

Paul here compares *giving* to *sowing*, and *receiving* to *reaping*. His point is that if we wish to reap, we must sow first. The example of the farmer enforces this point. Every time a farmer sows his field, he is exercising faith. He is believing that the seed he is planting in the field is going to come back multiplied.

It is precisely the same with our giving as Christians. If we want to reap, we first have to sow. Furthermore, the measure in which we sow will determine the measure in which we reap. If we sow sparingly, we will reap sparingly. If we sow bountifully, we will reap bountifully.

We can take the example of the farmer one step further. Sowing is not random scattering wherever we happen to be. If we were to walk down Main Street, scattering seed right and left into the gutter, we would not reap much of a harvest. Yet some Christians give like that. On random impulses, without prayer or principle, they just throw their money anywhere. It is no small wonder that they do not reap the benefits promised in Scripture.

Contrary to that picture of random scattering, responsible sowing means we select the best soil, we make the best preparation, we choose the right time, and we sow the best seed. That is precisely how we should handle our finances—both individually and collectively. We should select the best investment for the extension of God's Kingdom, we should make prayerful preparation, we should carefully follow the principles laid down in God's Word, and we should give of our best. In short, we should do everything in our power to secure the maximum return on our investment.

Giving with Purpose

Because it is of grace, God's Word teaches that nobody is forced or compelled to give. This is a grace gift. If it were under the Law, then not giving would make us lawbreakers. But as it is under grace, no one dictates to us.

You are not compelled to give under grace. I like that the Scripture says, "*as he purposes in his heart,* so let him give." So many of God's people are quite purposeless in their giving. Here is what they do. The offering plate comes along and they put their hand in their pocket. They look for a coin rather than a bill—that is for sure. The first coin they find is too big, so they feel around, looking for a smaller one, that turns out to be a nickel. But there is no purpose in giving like that, is there? You cannot say that person has purposed in his heart to give anything. It is just a hit-or-miss kind of business. It is a terrible failing to be purposeless in your giving. "Let each one give as he purposes in his heart."

We generally have no problem in believing that the words of Galatians 6:7 apply to other actions: "Do not be deceived, God is not mocked; for whatever a man sows, that he will also reap." If, for instance, a person sows unkindness and criticism, we would be sure to point out, "You'll reap unkindness and criticism." Or we could tell a person on the other hand, "If you sow love and good deeds, you will reap love and good deeds." We all understand that it does not mean merely the literal sowing of physical grain. We all know that, there is no question about it. But some of us have been so blind for so long that we have not seen that it applies equally in the financial realm. "Whatever a person sows, that he or she will also reap."

I hope you will believe me when I say that if you sow five-cent pieces, you will reap five-cent pieces. If you sow ten-cent pieces, you will reap ten-cent pieces. If you sow five dollar bills, you will reap five dollar bills. If you sow fifty dollar bills, you will reap fifty dollar bills. That is exactly it. Precisely as true and as literally real as in the agricultural realm, so it is in the financial realm. We sow and we reap. This is God's provision to make His grace abound toward us financially. We learn to sow in faith and we reap in faith. Multitudes of God's people have found this true.

Sowing in Faith

Years ago, I was listening to a dear Baptist preacher who was describing his ministry—how he had overworked, become sick and had a breakdown. With a wife and a family to support, he had gotten to the stage where he had only a little money—and a mounting pile of bills. One day he went out into the woods alone to have this out with God and settle it. As he wrestled in prayer with God, God spoke to him clearly and said, *Give your way out of this problem. Give your way out.* In other words, operate in faith.

So he went back and counted what he had—just under seven dollars. That was all. And he thought of a very good place to give it. He knew of a missionary in South America who was doing a fine job, so he went to the post office and arranged to send a money order. Well, he could not send a money order for the whole amount because he had to pay for the money order and the postage, so he worked it out with the postal clerk so that what he sent was all he had when the stamps and the postal order were paid. Then he had nothing.

That was in the morning. In his testimony he said, "By that night I had five hundred dollars in my pocket. And that was just the beginning!"

Faith Must Be Involved

This type of giving must be by faith. "Whatever is not of faith is sin." When you give, but not in faith, you are just playing with God. It is sinful. When you give lightly, casually, indifferently, just reaching into your pocket and seeing what comes out, you are really playing with Almighty God. I do not say this to bring condemnation, but to help you see the nature of this act.

For me, the offering is one of the most reverent parts of the service. I never give casually. If I do not feel like giving, I will give nothing. But you would never see me put five cents in an offering to God. God deals with me the way I deal with Him. Do I want Him to deal with me on a five-cent basis? No, I don't. You can be sure I don't. Do you?

This principle of faith is all through the Bible. Let's look again at the words of Hebrews 11:6: "He who comes to God must believe that He is, and that He is a rewarder of those who diligently seek Him."

This applies to finance. If you diligently seek God with your finance, He will reward you. You must believe that principle before you come to God—otherwise you cannot come to Him. Without faith it is impossible to please Him.

Clean and Crisp

The following is a true story from my experience. I know it to be true and my wife was a witness to it. When we were living in London and we did not have very much money, I opened my wallet one day to find three absolutely new one-pound notes. (In those days a pound was worth something!) Sometimes when you get money from the bank it is so clean and crisp the bills stick together. When I pulled out those pristine bills, the serial numbers were in order one after another.

I had no idea where those new bills had come from. I finally concluded that our daughter, who had just started a nursing job, possibly had brought home a little gift out of her first salary and slipped it into my wallet. Though that seemed unlikely, I knew there was no other possibility. She was a good giver, and I could think of no other way it got there. So I went to her and I said, "Kirsten, I want you to know I really appreciate that little gift of yours." From her expression, I could tell she had no idea what I was talking about. I thought of every possibility, but in the end there was only one conclusion I could come to: Almighty God put those three one-pound notes in my wallet.

Now, you may think that is stretching it, but that is my firm conviction. If God could put a coin in a fish's mouth, He could put three new pound notes in my wallet. I did not expect it. I was astonished. It took me a long while to absorb it, but He did it.

Some people say that money is unclean, but I will tell you that those three pound notes were beautifully clean. When money comes out of the mint, it is one of the cleanest things you can touch. What makes money dirty is the way it is handled.

In other words, money is neither clean nor dirty except according to the way it is used. Use all that God gives you in an attitude of faith. As you sow appropriately, you can be sure that you will reap. Let's learn more about giving, our third condition for receiving God's abundance.

16

Honoring through Giving

A third condition for receiving God's abundance is that we honor both God and our fellow man by what we give. The principle is this: *Giving of our substance* (our finance or whatever) *is a way ordained by God to honor both God and others.* Many Christians have failed to grasp the truth that there is actually a requirement in the way we use what we have received. We honor through giving.

In Romans 13:7 Paul makes it very clear that there are those to whom we owe honor: "Give everyone what you owe him: If you owe taxes, pay taxes; if revenue, then revenue; if respect, then respect; if honor, then honor" (NIV). We are all familiar with the idea of owing taxes or revenue. But Paul also says we may owe respect and honor—and whatever we owe, we are obligated to pay it. One way that we pay the honor we owe is by the way we handle our finances. Scripture reveals four different kinds of persons to whom we should render honor.

Honor God

First, we are required to give God His portion. "Honor the LORD with your possessions [substance], and with the firstfruits of all your increase; so your barns will be filled with plenty, and your vats will overflow with new wine" (Proverbs 3:9–10).

We give God the first and best of everything—the firstfruits. The scripturally appointed way to make sure we do that is to give the Lord the tithe, the first tenth of all our income. If we do this, He has promised to bless and prosper that which we retain for ourselves. "Your barns will be filled with plenty, and your vats will overflow with new wine" (Proverbs 3:10). That is abundance, and it begins with honoring the Lord with our wealth—bringing Him the first and the best of that which we have in the area of finance and our material possessions.

Let me point out something that is clear by implication: We can either honor the Lord with our wealth or we can dishonor Him. Really, we have only those two possibilities. If we do not give to Him abundantly and freely, we are dishonoring Him. But if we honor Him, it will come back to us in abundance.

Going back to the Old Testament, we find a number of related principles that govern our financial dealings, with special reference to the giving of our tithes to God.

Let's first take a moment to explain what is meant by the word *tithe*. It is such an old-sounding Anglo-Saxon word that some people might even not know what it means. The tithe is the first tenth of the income you receive. God is so wise that He knew some people would find it difficult to divide by some numbers, so He gave us the number ten to divide by. So, if you earn $750 a week, you just move the decimal point one place to the left and your tithe on that amount is $75. What could be easier?

If we combine what Scripture tells us explicitly in Leviticus 27:30, along with other references in the book of Numbers as well as other books like Malachi, God is essentially saying, "The tithe is Mine. It belongs to Me." In that light, it is not accurate to say you *give* your tithes to God. You *pay* them—you owe them. The tithe is the basis—the foundation of Christian giving. Then come the offerings, which are what you choose to give. Offerings are over and above what you owe. God says to

His people, "You've robbed Me, first of all, in your tithes and then in your offerings."

> "Will a man rob God? Yet you have robbed Me! But you say, 'In what way have we robbed You?' In tithes and offerings. You are cursed with a curse, for you have robbed Me, even this whole nation. Bring all the tithes into the storehouse, that there may be food in My house, and try [prove] Me now in this," says the LORD of hosts, "if I will not open for you the windows of heaven and pour out for you such blessing that there will not be room enough to receive it. And I will rebuke the devourer for your sakes, so that he will not destroy the fruit of your ground, nor shall the vine fail to bear fruit for you in the field," says the LORD of hosts; "and all nations will call you blessed."
>
> Malachi 3:8–12

The following points derived from this Scripture are significant:

1. Unfruitfulness in handling our finances brings us under a *curse*. In fact, it is part of the curse from which Christ offers us deliverance.
2. As always in Scripture, *faith is essential*. We are required to bring our tithes before we receive the promised blessing. God says, "Try Me now in this," that is, by bringing our tithes. This passage offers us no other way in which to qualify for the blessing.
3. The act of faith that God requires is *in the material realm,* and the blessing He promises is likewise *in the material realm*. I have been in prayer meetings where Christians pray, "Lord, open the windows of heaven and pour out a blessing." It sounds good, but I always want to shake them and say, "Listen, the blessing doesn't come by praying. It comes by tithing!" We can pray forever, but *if we don't bring our tithes, we have no claim to the blessing it ensures.*

The above passage from Malachi tells us one thing: that God keeps accounts. It was fifteen hundred years before the time of

Christ that Moses laid down for Israel the ordinance of tithing. It was about three hundred years before Christ came that Malachi brought his message to God's people. So God had been keeping a record for twelve hundred years. He did not forewarn them, but one day He came out with His reckoning. He said, "You've been robbing Me. And the result is instead of being blessed as I would like to bless you, I've had to put a curse upon you." I want to tell you the truth, friend, God keeps a reckoning of every one of us. He knows just how much we have given to Him all our lives.

And in Romans 14:12 it says: "So then each of us shall give account of himself to God." The word that is used for "give an account" in the Greek means primarily, but not exclusively, "a financial account." One day every one of us as a believer in Jesus Christ is going to have to give an account of what we have done with our finances. As far as I know, I will be happy in that day, and it does not worry me. Since the day that God saved me, He has never had less than a tenth of my total income. As a matter of fact, He has had much more. I say this not to boast, but to ask, What would be the good of teaching this if I didn't practice it myself? And I will tell you something else. I would be afraid to stop tithing, because I know what it has done for me. You see, God says, "You move in the material; I'll reply in the spiritual." This is faith.

I want to point out as well that the benefits of tithing are national. This is very, very true. Where Christians tithe regularly, God blesses the whole nation. To Israel He said, "You are cursed with a curse, *even this whole nation,* because you have been systematically robbing God." But on the other hand, He says, "Bring all the tithes into the storehouse and I will rebuke the devourer for your sakes. Your ground will bring forth its fruit in abundance and all nations shall call you blessed. For you will be a delightful land" (see Malachi 3:10–12, kjv). Notice, the curse is national; the blessing is national.

Some people will tell me, "Brother Prince, you're preaching the law." But I am not; I am preaching grace. Furthermore, the law of tithing did not originate with the Law of Moses. Don't imagine that. In Genesis 14:18–20, Melchizedek appeared to Abraham and blessed him, and in return Abraham gave to Melchizedek tithes of all. That was more than four hundred years before the Law of Moses. And Abraham is put forth in the Scriptures (see Romans 4) as a pattern to all who believe. Abraham is the father of all who believe—if we walk in his steps and his faith. One of the vital steps of the faith of Abraham was that when Melchizedek, the high priest of God, appeared to Abraham, Abraham gave to him "tithes of all."

It is very interesting because the epistle to Hebrews lays great emphasis on the fact that Jesus Christ is a High Priest after the order of Melchizedek. And it was a priest of the order of Melchizedek that appeared to Abraham. This priest of the order of Melchizedek gave to Abraham bread and wine—the two emblems of the communion. In return, Abraham gave to him tithes of all. And when at the Last Supper Jesus gave to His disciples the bread and the wine, He was telling them by that act, "I am a priest after the order of Melchizedek." Just as it is scriptural for us today to accept the communion emblems from the Lord, it is equally scriptural for us to bring the tithes to the Lord. The two things go together. Tithing is part of the priesthood of Melchizedek, and the Scripture says in Hebrews 7:24 that it is an unchangeable priesthood which never passes away.

The Levitical priesthood has passed away, but not the priesthood of Melchizedek. The Levitical priesthood under the Law of Moses was a subsidiary priesthood in which they received the tithes from God's people and then gave them to the Lord. But under the priesthood of Melchizedek God's people gave them directly to the priest. And in Hebrews 7 it says that Christ *receives* tithes—in the present tense, not in the past tense. Because we are under grace and not under the Law, it does not say that "Christ demanded tithes," but it says that "He receives them." Not merely did Abraham give tithes, but Jacob did too. You can read that in Genesis 28:22.

Tithing did not begin with the Law of Moses and it did not end with the Law of Moses. It is an unchanging pattern connected with an unchanging and eternal priesthood, the priesthood of Melchizedek. And Jesus Christ is a High Priest after the order of Melchizedek. He still receives the tithes of His people today.

If you have missed out on a lot of blessings, perhaps you are now beginning to understand why. You might be saying, "Could that be it? Could that be the dark shadow over my life? Could that be the reason why I don't have all the liberty and joy people talk about?" Maybe, dear friend, you have not been honoring God.

Honor Parents

Second, we are required to honor our parents with our giving. In Ephesians 6:2–4 Paul reminds us that the commandment to honor our parents is the first one that carries a promise with it. "'Honor your father and mother,' which is the first commandment with a promise: 'that it may be well with you and you may live long on the earth.'"

This commandment to honor our parents carries financial obligations with it. In Matthew 15, the Pharisees were criticizing Jesus for not keeping the traditions of the elders. Jesus in turn accused them of keeping the traditions of the elders but breaking the commandments of God. He gave one specific example:

> "For God commanded, saying, 'Honor your father and your mother'; and, 'He who curses father or mother, let him be put to death.' But you say, 'Whoever says to his father or mother, "Whatever profit you might have received from me is a gift to God"—then he need not honor his father or mother.' Thus you have made the commandment of God of no effect by your tradition."
>
> Matthew 15:4–6

123

Notice how we are to honor our parents: by giving them of our substance. If our parents are in financial need and it is in our power to help them but we fail to do so, then we are not giving them the honor which is their due. Out of long experience in counseling and deliverance, I can say with assurance that people who do not honor their father and mother never have it well with them.

Honor Servants of the Lord

Third, with our giving, we are required to honor the servants of the Lord who minister God's Word to us and who minister to our needs. In Acts 27 and 28 we read how Paul and his company endured on their journey to Rome. They escaped from a shipwreck onto the island of Malta. Arriving destitute in a rainstorm, they were received hospitably by the islanders. In due course, Paul began to minister to the sick on the island and many of them were healed.

Then, when the time came for Paul and his party to leave, the writer says that those who had been ministered to in this way "honored us in many ways; and when we departed, they provided such things as were necessary" (Acts 28:10). By supplying the financial and material needs of Paul and his party, these islanders rendered to them the honor that was due them for their ministry.

This is in line with what Paul himself says in Galatians 6:6: "Anyone who receives instruction in the word must share all good things with his instructor" (NIV). When people are instructed in the truths of God's Word, the Word of God itself requires that they honor those who instruct them—those who minister to them and pray for them—out of every good thing that God has given them.

Honor the Elders

Fourth, by our giving, we are required to honor the elders who govern us in the church. Paul says:

Let the elders who rule well be counted worthy of double honor, especially those who labor in the word and doctrine. For the Scripture says, "You shall not muzzle an ox while it treads out the grain," and, "The laborer is worthy of his wages."

1 Timothy 5:17–18

Clearly the honor that Paul has in mind is financial and material. The more faithful the elders are in their duties, the more careful we must be to see that they are remunerated in a way that expresses true honor.

Paul is speaking here of those who govern the Church—the elders, the presbytery, the leaders of God's people. He says, "If they're doing their job well, and especially if they're teaching the Word of God, they're worthy of double honor." To make this very clear and to be certain that everyone knows what he means by "double honor," he goes on in the next verse to explain: "The Scripture says, do not muzzle the ox while it is treading out the grain, and the worker deserves his wages." The honor Paul is speaking about there is not just nice words, not just words of appreciation, not just saying "thank you." It is a very real and material form of honor. It is increasing the wages or the financial remuneration of those who serve the people of God well in the Church.

We see, then, that we show honor by giving in four directions: to God, to our parents, to God's servants who minister to our needs, and to the elders who govern us in the Church. This is our third condition for abundance. It is significant that in English we often use the phrase, "to *pay* honor." If the honor we give to God or to others costs us nothing, we are not giving real honor.

17

Right Thinking, Speaking and Acting

The fourth condition for receiving God's abundance is *right thinking, speaking and acting*. First of all, I want to put the emphasis on thinking or meditating. It is impossible to think wrong and live right. Likewise, if you think right, you will inevitably live right. Note the instructions given to Joshua when he was given the task of leading God's people, Israel, into their inheritance in the Promised Land:

> "This Book of the Law shall not depart from your mouth, but you shall meditate in it day and night, that you may observe to do according to all that is written in it. For then you will make your way prosperous, and then you will have good success."
>
> Joshua 1:8

To me, that is the most complete promise of prosperity and success that a person could ever wish to receive. Let's look at it more closely.

Meditate, Confess, Do

As Joshua faced the tremendous task of bringing approximately three million people into their land, God gave him certain specific instructions. God told him, "If you follow these instructions, you'll be totally successful."

I like those two words put together in Joshua 1:8: *prosperous* and *successful*. That covers every kind of situation. If you are both prosperous and successful, there is no room for lack. There is no room for failure. God says, "If you will do certain things, then you will be prosperous and successful."

All the directions Joshua was required to follow are related to the Book of the Law. This was the total Scripture that was available in Joshua's time—what we call the Pentateuch and what the Jewish people call the Torah—the first five books of the Bible, the five books of Moses. That is what Joshua had. Bear in mind that today, it is granted to us to have 66 books. If Joshua could do well with just five books, consider how well you and I ought to be able to do with 66 books.

What are the basic requirements to receive it? *Meditate* in the law of the Lord. *Speak* the law of the Lord. *Obey* the law of the Lord.

First, we *meditate* in the law of the Lord day and night. Meditating is something we do in our minds.

Second, we don't let the words of the law of the Lord depart from our mouths. We *speak* it. We declare it. We ought to fill our conversations with the truths of this Book. The scriptural word for that is *confess*. *Confess* means saying the same with your mouth as God says in His Word. Do not talk about a lot of empty, trivial things. Do not give expression to unbelief and fear and doubt. Rather, express the truths of Scripture in your conversation.

Third, we must be careful to do everything written in it— doing and acting. We *obey* the law of the Lord. Once we have meditated, once we have spoken, then we do it. We do whatever it says. We apply it to every area of our lives.

What we think, what we say and what we do determine what we experience. I sum that up as follows: Think, speak and act God's Word.

The Promise of Prosperity

Anyone who chooses to do this—to think, speak and act God's Word—can be assured that the promise of prosperity will be given him or her without restriction.

> Blessed is the man who walks not in the counsel of the ungodly, nor stands in the path of sinners, nor sits in the seat of the scornful; but his delight is in the law of the LORD, and in His law he meditates day and night. He shall be like a tree planted by the rivers of water, that brings forth its fruit in its season, whose leaf also shall not wither; and whatever he does shall prosper.
>
> Psalm 1:1–3

Please read those last five words carefully! There is no room for failure or frustration there. Everything such a person does will succeed. Note that the condition for us to think, speak and act God's Word is emphasized in both negative and positive statements.

The negative statements, the actions we must *not* do, are given in verse 1. We must not walk in the counsel of the ungodly, nor stand in the path of sinners, nor sit in the seat of the scornful or mockers. Notice in that process that there is a gradual slowing down—from walking to standing to sitting. If we begin to walk in the way of the ungodly, then we will stand, and finally we will sit. At all costs, we must avoid that evil progression. Yet there are Christians who regularly accept the counsel of the ungodly in many areas of their lives. Then they wonder why they don't prosper. They are violating a primary negative requirement: We must not walk in the counsel of the ungodly.

Following the negative statements, there are two positive requirements. First, the successful person delights in the law of the Lord. We have to find our pleasure in God's Word. Does that sound difficult to you? I will tell you that the Word of the Lord is my delight. I enjoy it more than my daily food. I can remember times in my life when I was under tremendous pressure as a hospital attendant in the British army in North Africa. During those times, if I had to choose between breakfast and the Bible, I chose the Bible. I truly delighted in the Word of the Lord—and I still do. It is my source of pleasure, of satisfaction, of strength and of peace.

Second, the successful person meditates in it day and night. If I were to pick out one prescription in Scripture that is absolutely central to prosperity, it would be proper meditation. I will state again that whatever fills and occupies our minds will actually determine our experience.

On the basis of meeting this condition—to think, speak and act God's Word—the Bible says of any person, "Whatever he does shall prosper." Right now, as you read these words, determine that you will be such a person! Then go back over the verses given in this chapter. Read and meditate on them until they become a part of you. When that takes place, it will be natural for you to follow them.

18

Let God Add

Here is the fifth and final condition for prosperity: *Let God add—in His way and in His time.* Don't grab for abundance! Let God add it. Again, it should be the same in finance as in agriculture. We plant the seed, but God makes the harvest grow.

I remember years ago when I was in Ireland, I heard of a little boy of six whose parents gave him some potatoes to plant. He went out and planted his potatoes, and a week later he was out to see if they were growing. There was no sign of growth. Two weeks later he still saw nothing, so he dug them up to see if they were growing. In the end, he dug them up three or four times, and they never did grow!

Some Christians are like that. They plant their potatoes and then dig them up to see if they are growing. The essence of faith is that we let God do it. We meet the conditions, but God fulfills the promise.

Scriptural Encouragement

The following advice will give great security. Let God add to you in His way and His time. Strive after the Kingdom of God and let God add.

There are two Scriptures I would like to give you in this connection. The first is this: "All these blessings will come upon you and overtake you if you obey the LORD your God" (Deuteronomy 28:2, NASB).

I love that word *overtake* in the phrase "the blessings will overtake you, if you obey the LORD your God." In other words, you do not have to run after the blessings; you only need to cultivate obedience to the Lord. When you walk in the path of obedience to the Lord, then the blessings overtake you. That is the kind of prosperity that is desirable. That is the kind of wealth that has God's blessing with it. You are not seeking wealth. You are seeking to obey God. But because you are walking in the path of obedience, His blessings come upon you and overtake you.

The second Scripture is taken from the words of Jesus in Matthew 6:33: "But seek first [God's] kingdom and His righteousness, and all these things will be added to you" (NASB).

It is a question of priorities. What are we really seeking? Are we seeking wealth first? Then we cannot have God's blessings. But if we are seeking God's Kingdom and God's righteousness, then God guarantees that He will add to us all the things that we need, including the material things. Jesus said that you don't need to be too concerned about the material things—your Father knows you need them. But get your priorities right. Focus your mind and your will on obeying God and extending His Kingdom and going after His righteousness, and God will take care of all these things. We don't seek the "things"; we seek the "Kingdom." Then God adds all the "things" that we need.

I want to testify out of personal experience as I close this chapter. It really works. If we do our part, God keeps His side of the bargain.

By way of review, let's list again the conditions we have outlined for receiving God's abundance.

First, our motives and attitudes must be right.
Second, we must exercise faith.

Third, we must honor God, our parents, God's ministers and
  our spiritual leaders, by giving.

Fourth, we must practice right thinking, speaking and acting.

Fifth, we must let God add in His way and in His time.

If we meet these conditions, we can be certain that God's
abundance will overtake us.

PART 5

THE RIGHT
INVESTMENT

19

The Purpose of Provision

We will now focus on the end purpose of abundance. The last portion of 2 Corinthians 9:8 says, "That you, always having all sufficiency in all things, *may have an abundance for every good work.*" The purpose for which God supplies abundance is not merely selfish indulgence.

Don't get me wrong. I believe that God likes to see us enjoying His provision. It makes Him happy. But that is not the ultimate purpose. Rather, it is that we will have abundance for "every good work." The purpose of abundance is that we will be able to do everything God asks us to do with complete sufficiency.

One of the remarkable attributes of the Christians in the New Testament is that they never said, "If we have enough money, we will do this." They just said, "We will go here . . . we will go there . . . we will do this." Money really was not the question. Though they had much to say about money and were very practical in handling it, their plans did not depend on money. That is very different from the contemporary church, where so much of what is planned is dependent upon money.

I believe in being practical. I believe it is wise to make a budget and adhere to it. But some religious groups tie themselves down by their budgets. I do not believe God is going to be tied down in that way. In fact, God is not going to let us tie Him down in any way at all—by our rules, our systems, our theology or our finances.

The Primary Good Work

One specific good work for which God provides abundance is the primary "good work": *that we may provide Him a dwelling place*. The purpose of God from creation onward has been to dwell with man. We often talk as though the ultimate for us is to get to heaven. In reading the Bible, however, I find that the ultimate is to get heaven to earth. In the closing chapters of the Bible, we do not find earth going up to heaven; we find heaven coming down to earth. The ultimate thrust of God's purpose from creation onward is to dwell with man.

Consider two historic examples in the Bible where God asked His people, Israel, to provide for Him a dwelling place. The first dwelling place was the Tabernacle of Moses. The second was the Temple of Solomon. In each case God provided His people with abundance in advance, that out of their abundance they might return to Him all that would be needed to provide Him a dwelling place suitable to His glory.

God also gave very precise specifications as to the kind of dwelling place He wanted. He did not leave one measure or one material to chance. Everything was precisely specified, and everything was of the highest quality. There was nothing cheap or shoddy in anything that God required for His dwelling place. I believe that agrees with the very nature of God.

First, let's examine God's provision for the Tabernacle of Moses and the way it came about. Then let's look at God's provision for the Temple of Solomon and the way it came about. After that, we will conclude by giving an up-to-date application of these examples for you and me.

The Tabernacle of Moses

In Genesis God made a covenant with Abraham. He also gave him a preview of the captivity of Israel in Egypt.

> God said to Abram, "Know for certain that your descendants will be strangers in a land that is not theirs, where they will be enslaved and oppressed four hundred years. But I will also judge the nation whom they will serve, and afterward they will come out with many possessions."
>
> Genesis 15:13–14, NASB

The Living Bible says, "They will come away with great wealth." When God predicted the captivity of Israel in Egypt and their subsequent deliverance, He emphasized that when they were redeemed and delivered, they would come out with great wealth. This was not an accident. It was part of God's foreordained purpose.

We see this prediction fulfilled in Exodus 12. It came as the immediate result of the Passover night, when the families of the Israelites had been spared and every firstborn of the Egyptians had been killed.

> Now the sons of Israel had done according to the word of Moses, for they had requested from the Egyptians articles of silver and articles of gold, and clothing; and the LORD had given the people favor in the sight of the Egyptians, so that they let them have their request. Thus they plundered the Egyptians.
>
> verses 35–36, NASB

The Living Bible says, "They stripped the Egyptians." The fact is that the Israelites took everything the Egyptians had—gold, silver, raiment. Anything they set their eyes on and asked for, they got. Why? Because the Egyptians were so frightened that all they wanted was to get rid of these people, no matter what it cost.

You might ask, Was that just? I want to tell you that God is always just. He is more just than we think He is. Throughout the years of Israel's slavery in Egypt, God had been keeping a reckoning, and He reckoned that the Israelites were due a couple hundred years' worth of back pay. So they collected in one night. That is justice! A lot of people would not see it that way because they do not keep the same kind of reckoning that God keeps.

Complete Redemption

There is a beautiful description of the deliverance of Israel out of Egypt in Psalm 105:37: "He also brought them out with silver and gold, and there was none feeble among His tribes."

Redemption makes total provision for the needs of the redeemed. For Israel in Egypt, it all came through faith in the blood of the Passover lamb. That faith released the supply of every need—spiritual, physical and material. When those three million people marched out of Egypt not one of them limped, not one of them hobbled, not one of them used a cane or a crutch. In the church today we have a long way to go to attain that standard, but I believe it is God's standard. I believe redemption is complete, and that it covers every area of our lives.

Redemption is also very practical. How were the Israelites ever going to travel through the wilderness if they were sick or crippled? Bear in mind that they had been slaves. They had not had the best food or medical care. They were also very poor. But when God redeemed them, He took care of everything in one act. Those Israelites came out healthy and wealthy, with an abundance of gold and silver and everything that was precious.

The Purpose of Plunder

We must understand, however, that God had a purpose in all this. God gave Moses the plan for the Tabernacle where He was going to dwell in the midst of His people. Then He told Moses that *the people* were to provide the material and labor to build the tabernacle.

> And Moses spoke to all the congregation of the children of Israel, saying, "This is the thing which the LORD commanded, saying: 'Take from among you an offering to the LORD. Whoever is of a willing heart, let him bring it as an offering to the LORD: gold, silver, and bronze; blue, purple, and scarlet thread, fine linen, goats' hair; ram skins dyed red, badger skins, and acacia wood; oil for the light, and spices for the anointing oil and for the sweet incense; onyx stones, and stones to be set in the ephod and in the breastplate. All who are gifted artisans among you shall come and make all that the LORD has commanded.'"
>
> Exodus 35:4–10

The people were to bring their offerings out of the abundance God had provided for them through redemption to make the kind of dwelling God required. He gave them no options about the dwelling place. There was to be gold, silver and bronze. Everything had to be made just the way He required. His requirements were not unreasonable, however, because He had already given them everything they were going to need to comply with His directions.

Furthermore, God provided His people with the skills they would need to make the best use of all these materials. This He did by filling Bezalel with the Holy Spirit in such a way that he became a master craftsman, able also to instruct and oversee the other craftsmen whom God joined to him (see Exodus 35:30–35). The result is described in Exodus 36:2–7:

> Then Moses called Bezalel and Aholiab, and every gifted artisan in whose heart the LORD had put wisdom, everyone whose heart was stirred, to come and do the work. And they received from Moses all the offering which the children of Israel had brought for the work of the service of making the sanctuary. So they continued bringing to him freewill offerings every morning. Then all the craftsmen who were doing all the work of

the sanctuary came, each from the work he was doing, and they spoke to Moses, saying, "The people bring much more than enough for the service of the work which the LORD commanded us to do." So Moses gave a commandment, and they caused it to be proclaimed throughout the camp, saying, "Let neither man nor woman do any more work for the offering of the sanctuary." And the people were restrained from bringing, for the material they had was sufficient for all the work to be done—indeed too much.

Notice the closing phrase *sufficient . . . indeed too much*. By definition, that is abundance.

Regrettably, we do not often see such a situation in modern congregations. The trouble was not that they did not have enough. The trouble was that they were bringing so much they did not know what to do with it. That is God's abundance and the purpose for which it is given.

Redemption provides abundance. But the goal of redemption is a place for God to dwell among His people. And out of what God gives us through redemption, He asks us to give back to Him that which will provide His dwelling place.

The Temple of Solomon

David is first presented to us in Scripture in a very humble setting—the youngest son in a family of little wealth, out on the rocky mountains of Judah, looking after his father's sheep (see 1 Samuel 16:6–13). Yet, before his death, he bequeathed to the house of God—to the Temple that Solomon was to build—a staggering amount of riches out of his own private fortune.

One very significant realization we need to make is that during the reign of David there was a fantastic increase in the wealth of Israel. I do not know any way to calculate it, but their gross national product must have been multiplied hundreds of times over. What had been a poor, struggling nation that made its living out of agriculture, husbandry, cattle and sheep had become fantastically wealthy by the end of David's reign.

That was no accident. Israel's wealth was partly the result of God's blessing on David. We know that whenever God finds a person after His own heart to lead His people, He will bless His people through that person. But apart from that, God had a further purpose. At the end of David's reign, God wanted Israel to be ready for the construction of the Temple Solomon was to build. Again, God's goal was a dwelling place where He could be among His people. As with the Tabernacle, every detail of that dwelling place was precisely defined. Nothing was left to the imagination of the builder.

The account of what was given for the construction of Solomon's Temple contains some of the most glorious language found anywhere in writing. There is something breathtaking about the words David uses to describe the preparation he had made for the Temple:

> "Now for the house of my God I have prepared with all my might: gold for things to be made of gold, silver for things of silver, bronze for things of bronze, iron for things of iron, wood for things of wood, onyx stones, stones to be set, glistening stones of various colors, all kinds of precious stones, and marble slabs in abundance."
>
> 1 Chronicles 29:2

Notice the closing word of David's description—*abundance*. It sums up the provision made for the Temple just as it summed up the provision made for the Tabernacle. Abundance is, in fact, the level of provision that God always makes for His people. There is nothing limited or stingy about it. He is the God of abundance.

David then continues:

> "Moreover, because I have set my affection on the house of my God, I have given to the house of my God, over and above all that I have prepared for the holy house, my own special treasure

141

of gold and silver: three thousand talents of gold, of the gold of Ophir."

verses 3–4

It is difficult to find an accurate equivalent in our modern monetary system for a talent. I would say, however, that a talent of pure gold of Ophir was worth at least $1.9 million, probably a good deal more. So out of his own personal fortune, David provided the equivalent in gold of about $5.8 billion. That does not include the silver or the other materials.

Further on, we read what the leaders also gave out of their own private possessions:

Then the leaders of the fathers' houses, leaders of the tribes of Israel, the captains of thousands and of hundreds, with the officers over the king's work, offered willingly. They gave for the work of the house of God five thousand talents and ten thousand darics of gold, ten thousand talents of silver, eighteen thousand talents of bronze, and one hundred thousand talents of iron.

verses 6–7

According to my calculation, the figures in this passage amount to $9.7 billion worth of gold. Between them, David and the elders gave the equivalent of $15.5 billion of gold out of their own private fortunes. This is apart from the silver, precious stones, wood, marble and all the other items contributed as well. We need to remember in all this that David started as a little shepherd boy on the rocky hills of Judea.

God's Ultimate Dwelling Place

The upsurge in the economy of Israel that made possible the building of the Temple did not take long—fewer than seventy years, in fact. I want to suggest that something similar is happening today. We can talk about economic problems and moan

142

about prices, but actually there has never been so much money available anytime in the world as there is now. Not only that, but I find that God is beginning to open up undreamed of levels of prosperity to His people—to those, that is, who will respond to the revelation that the Holy Spirit is imparting.

I believe God is doing a work in our day that parallels what He did for Israel in the days of David, because God has a *purpose*. What is that purpose? He wants a dwelling place. He wants to dwell with man. And He is very precise about the specifications of His dwelling place. He is not stingy. He wants everything of the highest quality.

Granted, the dwelling place being constructed for God in this age differs in kind from both the Tabernacle and the Temple. The distinctive character of God's dwelling place today is described by Paul in 1 Corinthians 3:16–17:

> Do you not know that you are the temple of God and that the Spirit of God dwells in you? If anyone defiles the temple of God, God will destroy him. For the temple of God is holy, which temple you are.

In a similar way, Peter says in 1 Peter 2:5: "You also, as living stones, are being built up a spiritual house, a holy priesthood." We are talking here about God's ultimate dwelling place, which is not made of gold or silver or of any of the marvelously precious materials that were lavished on the Tabernacle of Moses or the Temple of Solomon. There is something infinitely more precious to God, and that is *people*. When God wants the most precious dwelling place of all, He chooses one made up of people, not materials. *And we are the people!* We are God's dwelling place! If God was so particular and so lavish about the Tabernacle and even more so about the Temple—both of which were temporary buildings—do you think He will be less particular or less lavish about His ultimate, eternal dwelling place, which is you and me?

Completing this dwelling place will require both labor and expense far beyond all that went into Solomon's Temple. The living stones whom God has chosen must be quarried from all nations on the face of the earth, for God will not be satisfied until "all nations, tribes, peoples, and tongues" are represented (Revelation 7:9). God has ordained, therefore, that "this gospel of the kingdom will be preached in all the world as a witness to all the nations" (Matthew 24:14).

I believe there is a reason these examples of the Tabernacle and the Temple are given in the Old Testament. God wants us to understand how much it is going to cost to complete His ultimate dwelling place in this age. We know, of course, that we cannot pay for our redemption, nor can the salvation of a soul be measured in terms of finance. But if we take seriously our responsibility to present the Gospel of the Kingdom to the billions of people of today's world, it is only practical to acknowledge that it is going to cost billions of dollars. Literal dollars. It is utterly unrealistic to talk about getting the job done without finances.

Filling the Temple

God's provision that is needed for this ultimate dwelling place is revealed in Haggai 2:6–9. (In Hebrews 10 this is quoted and specifically applied to the close of this age.)

> "For thus says the LORD of hosts; 'Once more (it is a little while) I will shake heaven and earth, the sea and dry land; and I will shake all nations, and they shall come to the Desire [wealth] of All Nations, and I will fill this temple with glory,' says the LORD of hosts."
>
> Haggai 2:6–7

What temple? God's dwelling place. The Lord is not talking here about the temple that was built in the days of Haggai, because that temple was destroyed nineteen centuries ago. He is talking about the close of this age and His dwelling place at this time. (See also Hebrews 12:25–29.) The Lord says, "I will fill this temple with glory." But first He says the wealth of the nations is going to come, to provide all that will be needed to build a house suited to His glory.

The statement that follows in verse 8 is extremely important: "'The silver is Mine, and the gold is Mine,' says the LORD of hosts." Bear in mind that the word *silver* in modern Hebrew is "money." The devil has no legitimate claim to any wealth at all. He is a thief. We do not have to plead with the devil for money. All we have to do is pry it loose from his dirty fingers, because he has no right to it.

When Jesus died and rose from the dead, all the treasures of this entire earth became legitimately His. He is the heir of all things, and we are co-heirs with Him. We share the inheritance. So in actual fact, we have a legitimate right to the silver and the gold through Jesus Christ.

Greater Glory

Continuing on with what God says in this passage from Haggai 2, in verse 9 God returns to the theme of the glory:

> "'The glory of this latter temple [the ultimate house of God] shall be greater than the former,' says the LORD of hosts. 'And in this place I will give peace,' says the LORD of hosts."

Again, it is very obvious that this mention of the temple is not a reference to the temple that was built in the days of Haggai. That temple perished in war. Rather, it refers to the dwelling place of God at the close of this age. What is God's dwelling place at the close of this age? You and me. His people. His completed Church. His Body. The Lord promises that for the purpose of building that dwelling, the wealth of the nations will come.

Let's look at one last picture in Isaiah. Again, these words are spoken to God's people at the close of this age.

"Arise, shine; for your light has come, and the glory of the LORD has risen upon you. For behold, darkness will cover the earth and deep darkness the peoples; but the LORD will rise upon you and His glory will appear upon you. Nations will come to your light, and kings to the brightness of your rising. Lift up your eyes round about and see; they all gather together, they come to you; your sons will come from afar, and your daughters will be carried in the arms. Then you will see and be radiant, and your heart will thrill and rejoice; because the abundance of the sea will be turned to you, the wealth of the nations will come to you."

Isaiah 60:1–5, NASB

Once again, there is a direct connection between the revelation of God's glory and the wealth of the nations. God's purpose is to have a dwelling place suited to His glory. For this purpose, He will make available to His people the wealth of the nations.

Do you believe that applies to us today? I do! Why will we need this wealth? So we can complete the dwelling place of God, which is made up of living stones. People. Millions and millions of people, many of whom have not yet been reached even once with the Gospel of Jesus Christ.

It will cost a lot. It will cost lives. It will cost time. It will cost money. It will cost everything we have. But God will make all abundance available to us for the work of completing His dwelling place.

20

Investing in People

To illustrate the way God wants us to use all that He provides for us, let's look now at a very unusual parable that Jesus related—the Parable of the Shrewd Manager. It is sometimes known as the Parable of the Unjust Steward. What is unusual about this parable is that Jesus takes an example of a man who did something that was unethical and wrong. Yet, in a certain sense, Jesus holds that man up as an example that we should follow.

The Shrewd Manager

Let's look at the parable first, and then I will try to show you in what way this man is an example for us to follow, specifically in the use of money. The parable is found in Luke 16:1–9:

> Jesus told his disciples: "There was a rich man whose manager was accused of wasting his possessions. So he called him in and asked him, 'What is this I hear about you? Give an account of your management, because you cannot be manager any longer.'
> "The manager said to himself, 'What shall I do now? My master is taking away my job. I'm not strong enough to dig,

and I'm ashamed to beg—I know what I'll do so that, when I lose my job here, people will welcome me into their houses.'

"So he called in each one of his master's debtors. He asked the first, 'How much do you owe my master?'

"'Eight hundred gallons of olive oil,' he replied.

"The manager told him, 'Take your bill, sit down quickly, and make it four hundred.'

"Then he asked the second, 'And how much do you owe?'

"'A thousand bushels of wheat,' he replied.

"He told him, 'Take your bill and make it eight hundred.'

"The master commended the dishonest manager because he had acted shrewdly. For the people of this world are more shrewd in dealing with their own kind than are the people of the light. I tell you, use worldly wealth to gain friends for yourselves, so that when it is gone, you will be welcomed into eternal dwellings."

NIV

The last verse is the application. These words of Jesus are addressed to us as believers, too. "I tell you, use worldly wealth to gain friends for yourselves, so that when it [the worldly wealth] is gone, you will be welcomed into eternal dwellings." It is based on the pattern of the shrewd manager. Because he was going to lose his job and was not going to be able to support himself any longer, he wanted the other people to welcome him into their homes. So he called them all in and reduced the debt they owed to his master. They were, in a sense, in his debt for that. Then, when he was fired from his job, he would be able to go and say, "Listen, I saved you four hundred gallons of olive oil, or two hundred bushels of wheat. So now receive me and take care of me, because I am no longer able to provide for myself."

How to Be Shrewd

That is the story—and Jesus refers to this manager as being *shrewd*. In fact, Jesus says, "The children of this world are much shrewder in their own area than the children of light."

Jesus commended this manager—not because he was dishonest, but because he was shrewd. In what way? He recognized that one day his strength and his resources would fail. That is also true of you and me. One day our strength and our resources are going to fail. One day we are not going to be able to work. One day maybe we will not be able to accept responsibility for ourselves.

So what did the manager do? While he still had money—and it wasn't his money but his master's money, though he had control of it—he invested it in people who would receive him when his own resources had failed.

Let me give you one piece of advice. Ultimately the best investment of money is in people, not in things. Bear that in mind.

Let's now apply this parable to our use of money as Christians. First of all, we need to realize that our money is not really ours. We are only managers. It is committed to us by God but it does not belong to us. We are in the same position as that manager.

Second, our money is only at our disposal for a limited time. One day we are going to be like the manager. We are going to come to the end of what we can do for ourselves.

Third, if we invest our money only in temporal things, we will have no eternal return from it. When we are fired from our jobs, in terms of the analogy, we will have nowhere to go. We will have spent our money and there will be nothing left of it.

Fourth, if we invest our money in the eternal welfare of other human beings, they will be there to welcome us when we pass from time into eternity. Jesus said, "They will receive you into eternal dwellings."

This is the real essence of this parable: that we can invest our money in people now, in time, in such a way that they will be in our debt. One day, when we pass out of time into eternity, they will be there to welcome us. They will say, "It was your money that made it possible for me to get to heaven. I am here before you to welcome you. Thank you for the way you used your money."

Can you see the principle? Invest your money in people and their eternal welfare. One day when you are out of a job and you come to the end of your own strength and your own resources, when you step out of time into eternity, there will be people there to welcome you. Why? Because you invested your money in people, not in things. Not in yourself, but in the eternal welfare of people. That is the best investment any of us can ever make of our money.

Let me briefly present three ways in which we can legitimately and scripturally invest our money in people.

Invest in the Poor

We can invest our money in helping the poor—especially the widows and orphans.

A few years ago, our office brought out a little booklet titled *Orphans, Widows, the Poor and Oppressed* (Derek Prince Ministries, 2000). The content of that book was somewhat astonishing to me. I had been preaching for well over fifty years and I had the impression that I knew most of what I would be preaching for the rest of my life. In those months after December 1998 when Ruth passed away, however, God gave me a new kind of compassion greater than I had ever had. So I put my heart into that message concerning the poor.

It came in much the same way as Psalm 84:6 describes: "When you pass through the Valley of Baca [that is, weeping], God will open a fountain." That is my revised version of that verse. With Ruth's death I passed through the valley of weeping and God opened that fountain. Something sovereign that only God could do—He gave me compassion. I became deeply concerned—I could almost say passionately concerned—about the people that our society neglects and treads underfoot: the orphans, the widows, the poor and the oppressed.

As I entered into this new understanding I was amazed at how much the Bible has to say about it. From beginning to the end this is a major theme of God's righteousness—whether it is in the patriarchs, under the Law of Moses, in the prophets or in the New Testament. Generally speaking, we as Christians have completely missed out on a vital area of our faith and our profession—which is to care for those whom no one else cares for.

A Standard of Righteousness

Let's look at Job, for example. In Job 31, we listen in as he rehearses a list of sins that he was not guilty of committing. (Many professing Christians, however, are guilty of these very sins.) Let's just look at a little from this chapter: "If I have kept the poor from their desire, or caused the eyes of the widow to fail, or eaten my morsel by myself, so that the fatherless could not eat of it. . ." (Job 31:16–17).

Notice the three groups there; the poor, the widows, the orphans. Job says, "If I haven't done what I ought to have done by them, I'm a sinner. I've failed in my basic obligations." Then he goes on to say—and he is affirming his own righteousness,

"(But from my youth I reared him as a father, and from my mother's womb I guided the widow); if I have seen anyone perish for lack of clothing, or any poor man without covering; if his heart has not blessed me, and if he was not warmed with the fleece of my sheep; if I have raised my hand against the fatherless, when I saw I had help in the gate; then let my arm fall from my shoulder, let my arm be torn from the socket."

Job 31:18–22

Job has not failed to care for the people who had no food or clothing or family to care for them. He was saying: If my arm has not been engaged continually in these acts of mercy and generosity, then it should not even be attached to my body.

That is a totally different viewpoint from that of most of us today. This was the standard of righteousness of the patriarchs before the Law of Moses and even before the Gospel.

The Call for Every Believer

I have come to see that God is requiring us to restore this kind of righteousness in the Church. In a way, I feel as though God gave me a task to proclaim this because—through no virtue of my own but nevertheless in obedience to God—I became the head of a family of twelve fatherless children. So people could not say to me, "You are preaching about something you've never done." Now the total number of my family members is more than one hundred and fifty persons.

I do not say this to claim any righteousness for myself. But I believe God in a sense charged me with the responsibility to confront the contemporary Church with its failure to do the basics. This is not something special for a few special people. This is something that God expects from every committed servant of His. Every believer. I envisage that if Christians as a whole, the Church, were to accept this responsibility and in genuine love and concern and compassion, reach out to the poor, the oppressed, the widows, the orphans, the people for whom the world does not care, I believe we would see a tremendous turning to God, because that is not what people associate with the Church. They associate the Church with religious buildings and sermons and "missionary offerings," but they do not see it working in the people that they run across every day.

This became an absolutely passionate burden with me. It quite surprised me to care so much, but I do. I cannot even think about it without beginning to cry.

I know that God touched my heart when He called Ruth home. He did something in me that changed much of my outlook and my priorities. That little booklet is the product of a deep dealing of God in my own heart and life. God has caused me to look at people with different eyes. I also found that I had become much less self-centered. I used to be so occupied with being right and doing the right thing and understanding scriptural truth that I could be very close to people who were in real need and not even be conscious of their need. But that began to change. And when I came in contact with people who were in need, who were suffering, I began to feel it. Then I began to respond to it.

I found that when you respond out of God's compassion to people's needs, it produces a very different response from when you are just "witnessing" or trying to "win souls." People are very suspicious of that. They really want to know what your motive is. But it is different if you approach them in real compassion—without any expectation of getting anything back or gaining church members or increasing your congregation. If you simply open your heart in real love and compassion to the poor, the afflicted, the downtrodden, the needy, they know it.

In the world today there is so much injustice. There is so very little real justice for the people who cannot afford lawyers and who cannot afford to take their cases to court, and who don't even know how to read legal documents. They are oppressed and they are taken advantage of continually. It is said that the rich are getting richer and the poor are getting poorer. If I were among the rich who are getting richer by neglecting the poor, I am sure that I would not have a good conscience.

Most of the Christians whom I know are rich in comparison to the rest of the world. We may consider ourselves poor, comparing ourselves with some other individual or particular class of persons. But in actual fact, if we compare ourselves with a multitude of the world today—the people of India, the people of China, the people of South America, vast areas of the earth—all of us are wealthy. And God is calling us to account for what we are doing with our wealth.

You can save a life, maybe from degradation and shame. You can perhaps provide a Christian home or a Christian education. That young boy or girl you support could turn out to be a servant of God who may one day win many souls for the Lord. And in eternity those souls will be credited to your account. It was your investment that made it possible.

Repay a Debt

Second, we can invest our money in people by repaying our debt to the Jewish people.

All Bible-believing Christians have this responsibility, but unfortunately it is one that many of us have neglected: our responsibility to the Jewish people. To understand this we need to begin with the words of Jesus Himself. In the gospel of John, Jesus is speaking to the Samaritan woman whom He met at the well of Jacob and He says: "You [Samaritans] worship what you do not know; we [Jews] know what we worship, for salvation is of the Jews" (John 4:22).

That is a basic statement of tremendous importance, especially coming from the lips of the Savior Himself. "Salvation is of the Jews." Maybe you have never really considered that. And yet if you do consider it, it is an indisputable historical fact. There is no other source of salvation but the Jewish people.

Suppose there had been no Jews in history. What would be the consequences? Let me suggest some of them. There would be no patriarchs, no prophets, no apostles. Bear that in mind—every apostle of the New Testament was Jewish. There would be no Bible—nearly every book in the Bible is authored by a Jew. And finally, no Savior because, remember, Jesus by His human birth is Jewish. How would we get on without patriarchs, prophets, apostles, the Bible or the Savior? It is obvious—there would be no salvation.

All Bible-believing Christians of all other races owe their entire spiritual inheritance to the Jewish people. We owe to them an incalculable debt. That one race is the channel through which God provided all those blessings to all other nations.

Showing Mercy

Many of us have overlooked that God today requires all of us to acknowledge our debt to the Jewish people and to do something about repaying it. Read what Paul says in Romans 11, as he is writing specifically to Gentile believers.

> For as ye [Gentile believers] in times past have not believed God, yet have now obtained mercy through their unbelief: Even so have these [Jews] also now not believed, that through your mercy [the mercy of the Gentiles] they also may obtain mercy.
>
> Romans 11:30–31, KJV

It was the unbelief of the Jewish people that caused them to reject Jesus and it was the rejection and crucifixion of Jesus that made salvation available to all other races.

The phrase *through your mercy* can be interpreted more than one way. It can be "through the mercy that you received from God" or it can be "through the mercy that you show in turn." I believe it means both. To us as Gentiles has been granted the mercy of God that came through the unbelief of the Jews; but also, as we receive mercy from God we are obligated to show mercy. We are obligated to show mercy to the Jews through whom His mercy came to us.

Further on, in Romans 15, Paul specifically applies this not merely to some spiritual repayment but to material and financial repayment of the debt. This is what he says, and he is speaking about an offering for the poor saints in Jerusalem, which he was collecting from the Gentile churches.

> For Macedonia and Achaia were pleased to make a contribution for the poor among the saints in Jerusalem [that is, primarily Gentile churches decided to make a gift of mercy to the poor Jewish believers in Jerusalem]. They were pleased to do it, and indeed they owe it to them. For if the Gentiles have shared in the Jews' spiritual blessings, they owe it to the Jews to share with them their material blessings.
>
> Romans 15:26–27, NIV

I wonder if you have ever noticed that passage, or heard it, or understood it. It is not just something that we do without any obligation, but we owe it. Let's read it again: "For if the Gentiles have shared in the Jew's spiritual blessings, they owe it to the Jews to share with them their material blessings."

Recognizing Sins Against the Jewish People

That assertion of what is owed to the Jews is right there in the New Testament. The unfortunate truth is that over many centuries multitudes of Christians, far from seeking to repay their debt to the Jews, have compounded it many times over. Many Christians today are lamentably ignorant of the past history of the Christian Church. Consequently, they do not realize the awful way in which we Christians have compounded our debt to the Jewish people.

The following extract from my booklet *Our Debt to Israel* brings this out:

> Few Gentile Christians are aware of the deeply ingrained, but seldom stated, attitude of the Jews toward them. The Jews have suffered persecution in many different forms from many different peoples, but—in their view of history—their cruelest and most consistent persecutors have been the Christians. Before we reject this view as untrue or unfair, let us glance briefly at the kind of historical facts upon which it is based.
>
> In the Middle Ages the Crusaders, on their way through Europe to "liberate" the Holy Land, massacred entire Jewish communities—men, women and children—numbering many hundreds. Later, when they did succeed in capturing Jerusalem, they shed more blood and displayed more cruelty than any of Jerusalem's many conquerors before them—except perhaps the Romans under Titus. All this they did in the name of Christ and with the cross as their sacred emblem. (For this reason I personally am never happy to see any genuine presentation of the Gospel described by the word *crusade*.)
>
> Later still, in the ghettos of Europe and Russia, it was Christian priests carrying crucifixes who led the mobs against the Jewish communities—pillaging and burning their homes and their synagogues, raping their women and murdering those who

sought to defend themselves. Their justification for this was that it was the Jews who had "murdered Christ."

Again, within living memory, the Nazis—in their systematic extermination of six million Jews in Europe—used as their instruments men who were professing Christians—mainly Lutherans or Catholics. Furthermore, no major Christian group, in Europe or elsewhere, raised their voices to protest or condemn the Nazi policy against the Jews. In the eyes of the Jews, multitudes of Christians stand condemned merely by their silence.

To undo the effect upon the Jewish people of these experiences—and countless others like them—will take more than tracts or sermons. It will require acts—both individual and collective—that are manifestly as kind and merciful as the previous acts were unjust and cruel.

Let's ask ourselves, simply and practically, What can we do to repay our debt to the Jewish people? I want to quote again from my booklet *Our Debt to Israel*.

First, we can express and cultivate an attitude of sincere love for Jewish people. Most standard forms of "witnessing" practiced by Christians do not reach the heart of the Jewish people at all. In fact, they frequently anger them and alienate them. But it is amazing how the apparently hard exterior of a Jew will melt when confronted by warm, unfeigned love. In nineteen centuries of dispersion among the other nations there is one thing that the Jews have seldom encountered—and that is love!

Secondly, in Romans 11:11 Paul says that "salvation is come unto the Gentiles, for to provoke them [Israel] to jealousy." This is another significant way in which we can repay our debt to the Jews—by enjoying and demonstrating the abundance of God's blessings in Christ in such a way that the Jews may be made jealous and desire what they see us enjoying.

Thirdly, the Bible exhorts us to seek the good of Israel by our prayers: "Pray for the peace of Jerusalem: they shall prosper that love thee."

Fourthly, we can seek to repay our debt to Israel by practical acts of kindness and mercy. In Romans 12:6–8 Paul lists seven different gifts which Christians should cultivate and exercise.

The last one he mentions is that of "showing mercy." I believe it is appropriate that we Christians exercise this gift not merely toward individual Jews, but toward Israel as a nation. Thus we would in some measure expiate the countless acts of injustice, cruelty and barbarity which have over the centuries been inflicted upon the Jews—often in the name of Christianity.

Bear in mind that what we do for the Jews will be reckoned as being done to Jesus Himself. In the story at the end of Matthew 25 when the King comes to judge the nations, He judges them by the way they have treated His brothers. Jesus says in Matthew 25:40: "The King will reply, 'I tell you the truth, whatever you did for one of the least of these brothers of mine, you did for me'" (NIV).

Whatever good we do for the Jewish people, with a right motive and with a pure heart, one day will be reckoned to our account as having been done to the Lord Jesus Himself.

Share the Gospel

The third way to invest our money in people is by taking the Gospel to all nations on earth.

This area of responsibility is one that extends literally to the ends of the earth: *our responsibility to all nations.* We begin with the final commission of Jesus as He gave it to His disciples after His resurrection at the close of Matthew's gospel.

> Then Jesus came to them and said, "All authority in heaven and on earth has been given to me. Therefore go and make disciples of all nations, baptizing them in the name of the Father and of the Son and of the Holy Spirit, and teaching them to obey everything I have commanded you. And surely I will be with you always, to the very end of the age."
>
> Matthew 28:18–20, NIV

That was really the final commission of Jesus. At the end of His earthly ministry what did He ask of His disciples?

He said: "Go and make disciples of all nations." But first of all He said: "All authority in heaven and on earth has been given to Me." By implication, He said: "Through My death and resurrection, I have obtained back for you the authority that was forfeited by man's transgression and fall. Now you are in a position to exercise that authority on My behalf and in My name." Then He said: "The way in which I want you to exercise this authority is to go and make disciples of all nations and then baptize them in the name of the Father, the Son, the Holy Spirit, and then teach them to obey everything I have commanded you."

He closed with these words: "Surely I will be with you always, to the very end of the age." There is a promise. But I do believe that promise really only applies to those who obey the command. He says: "Go and make disciples, and I will be with you." His continuing presence with us is really dependent on our being willing to go and do what He said.

The Destiny of Souls

At the end of Mark's gospel we have a similar commission. Jesus said to His disciples:

> "Go into all the world and preach the good news to all creation. Whoever believes and is baptized will be saved, but whoever does not believe will be condemned."
>
> Mark 16:15–16, NIV

That is a tremendous commission. The destiny of all souls in all the earth is in the hands of us as the disciples of Jesus. We have to go and present them with the opportunity to be saved. What they do with that opportunity is their responsibility, but our responsibility is to make the opportunity available to them. The way they respond to the Gospel message will determine their eternal destiny. But how can we answer to God if we never give them the opportunity to make that commitment to the Gospel?

The early disciples clearly understood what Jesus meant and they acted on it. The last two verses of Mark 16 say this:

> After the Lord Jesus had spoken to them, he was taken up into heaven and he sat at the right hand of God. Then the disciples went out and preached everywhere, and the Lord worked with them and confirmed his word by the signs that accompanied it.

verses 19–20, NIV

It is significant that Jesus sat down. He sat down because He had finished His task. This is emphasized also in the epistle to the Hebrews. After He had offered one sacrifice for sin forever He sat down (see Hebrews 1:3). He sat down because His responsibility was fulfilled. Then the responsibility of the disciples came into operation. When Jesus sat down, it was their turn to go out and begin to do what He told them to do. He had obtained for them, and for all mankind, the possibility of eternal salvation—forgiveness of sins, eternal life, acceptance with God. That was His responsibility; He had fulfilled it. Now He transferred the responsibility to His disciples and they understood what He meant. They went out and preached everywhere. And it says because they obeyed the commission of Jesus, God confirmed their words with signs that followed it.

Standing Orders

Some people say the signs do not follow today. Somebody made this rather pithy comment on that: "The signs don't follow because people don't go. The signs are not promised to those who sit in church pews. They are promised to those who go and preach the Gospel everywhere." Whoever said that also gave this little analogy: "It's hard to follow a parked car." So many Christians today are parked cars. Parked in some church pew, parked in some place where they accept no real responsibility for the rest of the world, where it is as though the words of Jesus had never been spoken.

I come from a military background, and I know at least one principle of military orders. When an order is given, it is never withdrawn, and is always in force until it is either canceled or replaced by another order. Nearly twenty centuries ago, Jesus said, "Go into all the world and preach the Gospel to all creation." Those orders have never been canceled: they have never been replaced. They are just as valid for us today as they were for the first disciples who heard them. And if the first disciples had not done what Jesus said, they would have been guilty of direct disobedience. If we do not do what Jesus says, we are guilty of direct disobedience just as much as they would have been.

Now we will go on to look at the very last words of Jesus spoken on earth before He was taken up to heaven. These are found in the first chapter of Acts. Scripture says this about His meeting with the disciples:

> So when they met together, they asked [Jesus], "Lord, are you at this time going to restore the kingdom to Israel?" He said to them: "It is not for you to know the times or dates the Father has set by his own authority. But you will receive power when the Holy Spirit comes on you; and you will be my witnesses in Jerusalem, and in all Judea and Samaria, and to the ends of the earth."
>
> Acts 1:6–8, NIV

Scripture says that when Jesus had finished speaking those words, He was taken up and a cloud received Him out of their sight. What were the last words He spoke? *To the ends of the earth.* I believe He intended those words to be imprinted on their minds with special force. The very last words they ever heard from His lips before He was taken out of their sight were *to the ends of the earth.* That is where the heart of the Lord was. He was concerned that the entire world should hear the Good News that He had died and risen from the dead and made salvation possible.

The disciples were concerned with prophetic themes. They wanted to know if this was the time for the Kingdom to be restored to Israel. Of course, that was a very important question to Jewish believers. He said: "Don't be too worried about that. You do what I tell you. You attend to your business; the Father will attend to His business."

Those words, again, are just as valid for you and me today as they were for the first disciples, and as we consider our obligation as Christians to carry the message of the Gospel to all nations and to the ends of the earth.

Paul says in Romans 1:14–15: "I am obligated both to Greeks and non-Greeks, both to the wise and the foolish. That is why I am so eager to preach the gospel also to you who are at Rome" (NIV).

Paul says he is obligated. In other words, he has a debt— a debt to Greeks (the educated), to non-Greeks (people who are not educated, who cannot read or write), to the wise (the sophisticated, cultivated, and talented), and to the foolish (the people who have nothing). Paul is saying, "It doesn't matter what kind of people they are. I don't have to decide whether they are worthy or unworthy, whether they're the kind of people who are likely to respond or not to respond." He says, "That's not my business. My business is to communicate the Gospel. What they do with it is their business."

Our Obligation

Those words do not apply only to Paul. They apply, in a measure, to every Christian. Every one of us is under an obligation. The Greeks, the non-Greeks, the wise, the foolish. It does not matter what kind of people. That is not our responsibility. Nor is it our responsibility what they do with the Gospel. That is their responsibility. But it is our responsibility to convey the Gospel to them.

We cannot all be evangelists, carrying the Gospel to the utmost parts of the earth. But we can all have a commitment to be involved. It is a collective responsibility of the entire Church of Jesus Christ.

Let's look at John's vision of the redeemed in glory found in the book of Revelation:

> And they sang a new song: "You are worthy to take the scroll and to open its seals, because you were slain, and with your blood you purchased men for God from every tribe and language and people and nation. You have made them to be a kingdom and priests to serve our God, and they will reign on the earth."
>
> Revelation 5:9–10, NIV

For many years it has been impressed upon me that when the company of the redeemed is complete, there must be representatives among them from every tribe and language and people and nation. The Church of Jesus Christ cannot be complete until there is at least one representative in it from every tribe, language, people and nation. If we invest our money in conveying the message of the Gospel especially to those tribes, languages and nations that have never yet received the Gospel, then out of them will come those who will be redeemed through their faith in Christ. And one day, in the presence of God in eternity, they will be reckoned to our account. They will be there to welcome us into eternal homes, because we wisely invested our money in people.

I want to ask you—what is your objective in living? What are you living for? Are you desiring God's abundance? Are you praying for God to supply all your needs? Do you realize why abundance is given to you? It is that you may share with others.

21

Give Yourself to God

As God blesses us with abundance, it follows naturally that we will have plenty to share, and this will be true in every area of our lives. But it all begins with an essential step, and that is the first point we make in this chapter.

Giving Begins with You

First and foremost, *our giving begins with giving ourselves fully to God*. You cannot buy God's favor by giving. You cannot buy salvation by giving. You cannot buy forgiveness of sin. The first step in being in right relationship with God is to give yourself to Him.

Paul says in 2 Corinthians 8:5 about the people at Corinth that "they first gave themselves to the Lord," then they gave of their substance. And this is the right order. First give yourself to God. May I ask you a question? Have you given yourself to God? If you have, you know that you no longer belong to yourself. If you have given yourself to God, you belong to God. Would you agree? You should be convinced. But you can't have it both ways. If you have given yourself to God, you are God's. All that you have is God's, too.

When we give ourselves to God, knowing that all we have is His, wonderful things begin to happen.

Giving Draws God's Love

Second, *our giving to God draws down God's love upon us*. When we give to God we focus God's love upon us. Second Corinthians 9:7 says, "God loves a cheerful giver." So if you want to be really sure that God loves you, what are you going to do? Give cheerfully.

I like the word *cheerful*. The Greek word is *hilaros* from which we get the English word *hilarious*. God loves a hilarious giver. I have seen God's people give hilariously, and strangely enough, they have been among the poorest people I have known. I have seen, for instance, the very poor in Africa come with a chicken, with eggs, with corn cobs or coffee beans, then decide it was not enough, and come back with some more. And there was a spirit of hilarity in their giving. They were having a wonderful time giving to God.

After David had sinned and repented, he said to God, "Uphold me with thy free Spirit" (Psalm 51:12, KJV). The word *free* in Hebrew is directly connected with the word that is used for "giving freely." The Holy Spirit is a Spirit who helps people give freely. When the Holy Spirit is ruling, you give hilariously. You enjoy giving. The Holy Spirit helps you enjoy your religion. Without the Holy Spirit, religion is a bore. Most people endure their religion. But people who are yielded to the Holy Spirit enjoy their religion—and part of their religion is their giving. You cannot separate that aspect.

Giving "Proves" Our Love

Third, *our giving is proof of our love*. Paul says this twice in 2 Corinthians 8:8: "I speak not by commandment, but I am testing the sincerity of your love."

That is a very searching statement, but every one of us knows immediately in our hearts it is true. It is all bluff if we talk about loving God yet are reluctant about giving. Such love is not sincere. But Paul says, "Here's a chance to prove the sincerity of your love."

Then, in the same chapter, speaking about the same theme, Paul says: "Therefore show to them, and before the churches, the proof of your love and of our boasting on your behalf" (2 Corinthians 8:24). People often say that giving ought to be done in private. Paul says to give publicly before the churches and make it the proof of your love.

I knew of a group that held the theory that your right hand ought not to know what your left hand is doing. So when they gave an offering, they put their left hands behind their backs holding a penny piece, which they then offered, singing at the same time, "All to Jesus I Surrender."

I said to myself, *I know why their right hand shouldn't know what the left hand was doing—because it would be embarrassed if it found out!* There is a lot of foolish talk about not doing things in public, but Paul says, "Show to them, the churches, the proof of your love by your giving."

In John's first epistle, he says: "My little children, let us not love in word or in tongue, but in deed and in truth" (1 John 3:18). If you are not willing to give to God, you are loving God only in word and in tongue but not in deed and in truth. Do not deceive yourself, because you are not deceiving God. Giving is the proof of the sincerity of our love.

Giving Brings Sufficiency

Fourth, *our giving means that all will have enough.* God has made the members of the Body of Christ dependent upon one another. It is true in the gifts of the Spirit: To one He gives a word of wisdom, to another a word of knowledge, to one He gives a tongue, to another an interpretation. God has fitted the whole Body so that it must be mutually dependent. This is true as well in every area including finance.

Paul says to the people in Corinth, "Now it is your turn to give to the poor saints in Jerusalem. They have a need, and you have more than enough. So now it's your turn." Then he said, "Another day may come when it will be their turn to give to you." He says, "I do not mean that others should be eased and you burdened; but that people may share out equally" (see 2 Corinthians 8:13–15). He goes on to say, do this "that there may be equality. As it is written, 'He who gathered much had nothing left over, and he who gathered little had no lack'" (2 Corinthians 8:14–15).

Paul is quoting from Exodus 16 about the children of Israel going out to gather the manna. You will recall that God made provision for their food through the manna that descended every morning early like the dew and lay round about the camp. Every Israelite had to go out each day and gather his manna. And God said that every individual was to have as much as he or she could eat and that the measure was to be an omer, which is simply a Hebrew measure.

So when they went out and gathered, they brought in what they had. Some had a lot, some had a little. But when they shared it out, they found that each one had exactly the right amount— an omer. Paul says this is how it should be with finance. Some may have a lot, some a little. But if the people who have too much will share with the others, we will find that everyone has enough. There will be equality. If we have too much and we do not share, somewhere or other our brothers or sisters are going to feel the burden.

Giving Establishes Righteousness

Fifth, *our giving completes and establishes our righteousness* that we have by faith in Jesus Christ. In 2 Corinthians, Paul quotes Psalm 112:9. The whole psalm is about the righteous, and Paul says, "As it is written, 'He has dispersed abroad, he has given to the poor; his righteousness endures forever'" (2 Corinthians 9:9).

What makes a person's righteousness permanent, firmly established? His or her giving. And this is absolutely true. It is our giving that finally sets the seal on our commitment to Jesus Christ.

A man once came to me and said he did not feel he was sufficiently zealous for the Kingdom of God. He asked me how he could be more zealous. I replied, "Brother, I'll tell you one simple way: Invest more in the Kingdom of God. Jesus said, 'Where your treasure is, there will your heart be also.' Put your treasure in; your heart will follow." And that is true.

Jesus did not make it so spiritual. He did not say, "Where your heart is, your treasure will follow." He said, "Where your treasure is, there your heart will be" (Matthew 6:21). Friend, if you want to be more zealous for church meetings, just invest a little more. If you want to be more zealous for missions, invest a little more. You will be amazed how much you care when you have invested. This is an eternal, unchangeable spiritual law.

Suppose a great big building burns down somewhere in the middle of a big city. We will all feel a sense of regret, but there are some who will be much more regretful than the rest: the people who invested in the building. Because their treasure is there, their hearts are there, too. When your treasure is in the Kingdom of God, your heart will be there. You cannot get around it.

Invest in the Kingdom of God and you will be committed to the Kingdom of God. Disperse and give, and your righteousness will remain forever. I have seen this with many new converts. They are never really established Christians until they learn to give systematically to God. This is one reason that so many young people and young converts are up and down in their faith—because they are not committed. One good way of being committed is giving systematically and liberally to the Kingdom of God.

It works. I have had several decades of experience in the ministry and I am talking about what I know. It works. People who are financially committed are well on their way to becoming established and stable; their righteousness will remain forever.

Giving Insures against Evil Times

Sixth, *our giving is an insurance against evil times.* I lived in Britain when a Social Security system was in operation. They gave you a card and you were required to get a stamp every week. At the end of the year, if you had 52 stamps on your card, one for each week, you had no problems with Social Security. If you got sick, somebody would care for you. If you were out of work, somebody would meet your needs. It was all arranged and it all depended on the stamp.

I want to tell you, God has a stamp system, too. You should keep your card stamped and up to date. If you give regularly, God accepts full responsibility for all your needs. Then if you have a need, you come to God and say, "My tithes are paid up to date. This is what I've given to missions. My card is stamped." God is much more faithful than the British government, believe me. You can trust Him. I am not saying that the British government is unfaithful—don't misunderstand me. But they have their limits. God is unlimited.

In Psalm 37:21, Scripture says: "The righteous shows mercy and gives." In verse 25, just a little further on, David says: "I have been young, and now am old; yet I have not seen the righteous forsaken, nor his descendants begging bread." But notice what comes first, "The righteous shows mercy and gives." *Then* David says, "I have not seen the righteous forsaken, nor his descendants begging bread." The righteous one has the stamp up to date on his card.

"Cast your bread upon the waters, for you will find it after many days. Give a serving to seven, and also to eight, for you do not know what evil will be on the earth" (Ecclesiastes 11:1–2).

Do you see that last sentence? "You do not know what evil will be on the earth." Get your card stamped up to date. Unemployment may be coming. Who knows? Give a serving to seven, that is the standard, and then give to another, to eight, just for a little extra insurance, for you do not know what is coming on the earth.

I read a book once by Oswald Smith, who years ago was pastor of the People's Church in Toronto, Canada. He gave the testimony of pastoring that church all through the Depression years, which swept right across Canada and the United States. Every day in his office all through that long period, men came in off the street for financial help because they were flat broke. He said he always checked with those men to see if they were up to date in their commitments to God. And he said that never in all those years did he ever have a man come in needing help who had paid his tithes. Never once. I tell you, I would be scared not to tithe. I mean that. You could not get me to stop.

Paul, writing to the church at Philippi, thanks them for a gift they have sent through Epaphroditus. He says:

> Indeed I have all and abound. I am full, having received from Epaphroditus the things sent from you, a sweet-smelling aroma, an acceptable sacrifice, well pleasing to God. [Notice the next word:] *And* my God shall supply all your need according to His riches in glory by Christ Jesus.
>
> Philippians 4:18–19, emphasis added

A lot of Christians quote Philippians 4:19 but they leave out the *and* connecting it to the previous verse. They say, "My God shall supply all your needs," but Paul put an *and* in front of that. He said, "You have acted in faith. You have given beyond what you felt you could afford." Then the *and* will come in: "*And* my God will see to it that you never lack." That promise is not for those who do not give. Absolutely not. It simply does not apply. It is only for those who give in faith. Then, Paul says, God will never let you down.

Giving by Grace with Faith

Seventh, *our giving is by God's grace, and by faith*. How do we appropriate grace? By faith. This is true of all salvation, including financial salvation. I can prove it to you from Psalm 78. In that psalm you will find a record of all God's provision for Israel—how He brought them out of Egypt, how He brought them through the Red Sea, how He led them by a cloud, how He fed them with manna, how He gave them water to drink out of the rock, how He ensured that they never lacked, their shoes never wore out, their clothes never got old, and every single need was met. Yet Psalm 78:22 says, "They did not believe in God, and did not trust in His salvation."

The word *salvation* is the biblical word for every provision of God's grace for His people—Old Testament and New Testament alike. The one all-inclusive word that sums it all up is *salvation*. Every principle that applies to salvation in general applies to all aspects of our giving.

The entire principle is laid out in Ephesians 2:8: "For by grace you have been saved through faith." The channel that brings God's grace into you is faith. Without faith you have no channel. God is pouring out His blessing but nothing comes your way because you do not have the channel. In order to receive grace, you have to put up the channel of faith. Then God's blessing comes cascading down your channel into your life—spiritual, physical and financial blessing. It is all salvation.

Just let me mention this. I counted twelve places in the Greek New Testament where the Greek word for *saved* is used specifically of physical healing. Healing is just one aspect of salvation—the physical aspect. Full salvation centers in one Person, Jesus Christ, who is the Savior, the Healer, the Deliverer, the Baptizer with the Holy Ghost. One of God's great unchanging, eternal covenant names (one of seven covenant names of Jehovah) is the Great Provider: *Jehovah-jireh*, "the LORD will Provide." Every one of those covenant names reveals an eternal, unchanging aspect of God's nature as "the LORD that changes not." He is the Provider just as much as He is the Savior or the Healer or the Deliverer or the Baptizer. And it is all included in this glorious salvation.

A prophetic word of the Lord was brought to me once when I was sick that said: "Consider the work of Calvary, a perfect work—perfect in every respect, perfect in every aspect." It is perfect in the financial aspect just as perfectly as it is in every other aspect. It is part of grace. It is received through faith. Grace comes by Jesus Christ. Jesus Christ on the cross became poor that we through His poverty might become rich. It is all through the cross; it is all by grace; it is all through faith.

In all that we have said in this last point, we observe this one great principle: *We must act in faith*. Faith without works is dead. Somebody has very finely expressed it: "Faith without corresponding actions is dead." Dead faith does not produce living results. Lots of people say they believe, but it's only words without actions. They just sit passively, inactive, doing nothing. It is dead faith, and they are dead Christians. Faith without works is dead. The Greek word is so vivid. It means "a corpse." It is almost revolting, and that is how faith is without works.

The Dangers of Fear and Unbelief

Do you really believe in God? If you really do, you cannot fail to be willing to act in faith with your abundance. If you do not act in faith, it is sheer unbelief. That is all it is. Just plain unbelief—and it is combined with fear. Two deadly, destroying, damning sins—fear and unbelief.

You may say, "Brother Prince, don't talk to me like that!" But let me tell you, friend, in Revelation 21:8, the first two categories of people that go into "the lake which burns with fire" are the cowardly (or fearful) and the unbelieving. And after them come the witches and the sorcerers and the murderers and the adulterers. But the first two categories of people headed for eternal damnation in the lake of fire are the fearful and the unbelieving.

172

What would keep you from giving yourself to God except fear or unbelief? Somebody once said to me, "You make things so plain." I certainly aim to make them plain. My aim is that no one turns away not knowing what I have been trying to communicate. That way, I will be able to say, "I have kept back nothing that was profitable to you. I have not shunned to declare to you all the counsel of God." (See Acts 20:27.) When Paul used the words *I have not shunned*, it indicated there would always be many pressures against a preacher not to tell the whole truth about some subjects.

I know a lot of board members and Christians who get mad when the pastor begins to preach about giving. But the people who never get mad when the pastor preaches about giving are the people who give regularly. They do not mind. They sit back and enjoy it. They say, "Praise the Lord."

Summary

I will now briefly recapitulate what we have covered so far in this chapter. We have been focusing on God's grace making full provision for us, and the corresponding grace in us that causes us to give hilariously to God. We pointed out that in the New Testament nobody dictates to you what you shall give. It is a personal decision you must make for yourself. "So let each one give as he purposes in his heart, not grudgingly or of necessity" (2 Corinthians 9:7).

Then we covered seven relevant factors to consider as you purpose to give of yourself and your resources to the Lord:

1. It begins with giving yourself.
2. Giving draws down God's love upon you. God loves a hilarious giver.
3. Giving is the proof of the sincerity of your love for God and His people.
4. When God's people share, all have enough.

5. Giving completes and establishes the righteousness that you have by faith in Jesus Christ.
6. Giving is insurance against evil times.
7. Giving is by grace, but it must be accompanied by faith.

In the realm of finances, the law of sowing and reaping applies as much as in any other realm. "He who sows sparingly will also reap sparingly, and he who sows bountifully will also reap bountifully" (2 Corinthians 9:6). It is a fact that cannot be changed.

Let me offer this counsel to you as you consider the principle of God's abundant provision. Practice giving. Make a resolution to be generous. Don't be stingy. Don't hold on and say, "I may not get any more." The measure with which you give out will be the measure that you receive back. Make up your mind as you face the prospect of an abundant life. Purpose in your heart that the grace of giving, accompanied by faith, is going to be in operation in your life.

A Personal Commitment

I want to conclude this book by giving you the opportunity to do exactly what we have discussed in this chapter. I want to lead you in a prayer by which you can give yourself to God. This could be a moment of life-changing importance to you as you commit yourself and your resources to the Lord.

As I have often said, I made it my aim long ago never to simply give nice religious lectures. I always want to provide an opportunity for you to respond. This is your moment to respond to all you have read in this book. If you want to commit yourself fully to the truths we have shared, please pray this following prayer out loud:

Dear Lord Jesus,

I come to You now by Your grace, and with faith in Your name. I want to commit myself fully to You at this moment, and I want to give You everything that I am and everything that I have. I confess that nothing I have is really mine. It is all a gift that has come from You. And now, I place it in Your hands, returning it to You with thanks. The same is true with me, dear Lord. I am not my own, but I have been bought with a price—Your precious blood. You have purchased me, and I give myself once again to You.

Dear Lord, as I place myself and all I own into Your hands, I ask that You would give me the grace and wisdom to steward what You have given to me. Help me to be a hilarious, generous giver. Help me to invest Your resources wisely. Help me to respond to the promptings of Your Holy Spirit as I share the resources with which You have blessed me. Help me to be aware of those among the poor, among Your people, the Jews, and among my brothers and sisters in the Church who are in need of the resources You are giving to me. Please help me to give in a way that brings glory and honor to Your name.

And for all the good and all the blessing that flows as a result, I will be careful to give You the honor, the praise and the glory—for only You are deserving of it.

All of me and all that I have and will have, I now commit to You in love and faith. In Your name I pray.

Amen.

Blessings to You

By offering that prayer, you have placed yourself totally in the hands of the Lord—a wonderful step of faith that He will surely reward. May you experience His favor and fruitfulness in the years ahead. May the Lord bless you richly as you experience the promise of His provision.

Subject Index

vanity, 88
victory, 30

want, 20
wealth, 8, 19, 22, 42, 90–92, 94,
    102–4, 107, 137
weariness, 33
widows, 150–51
wilderness, 73–74

wisdom, 92, 103
withholding, 111
witnessing, 157
word of knowledge, 166
word of wisdom, 166

"yes and amen", 65–67

zeal, 168

Scripture Index

Derek Prince (1915–2003) was born in India of British parents. Educated as a scholar of Greek and Latin at Eton College and Cambridge University, England, he held a Fellowship in Ancient and Modern Philosophy at King's College. He also studied several modern languages, including Hebrew and Aramaic, at Cambridge University and the Hebrew University in Jerusalem.

While serving with the British army in World War II, he began to study the Bible and experienced a life-changing encounter with Jesus Christ. Out of this encounter he formed two conclusions: first, that Jesus Christ is alive; second, that the Bible is a true, relevant, up-to-date book. These conclusions altered the whole course of his life, which he then devoted to studying and teaching the Bible.

Derek's main gift of explaining the Bible and its teaching in a clear and simple way has helped build a foundation of faith in millions of lives. His non-denominational, non-sectarian approach has made his teaching equally relevant and helpful to people from all racial and religious backgrounds.

He is the author of more than fifty books, six hundred audio and one hundred video teachings, many of which have been translated and published in more than one hundred languages. His daily radio broadcast is translated into Arabic, Chinese (Amoy, Cantonese, Mandarin, Shanghaiese, Swatow), Croatian, German, Malagasy, Mongolian, Russian, Samoan, Spanish and Tongan. The radio program continues to touch lives around the world.

Derek Prince Ministries persists in reaching out to believers in more than 140 countries with Derek's teachings, fulfilling the mandate to keep on "until Jesus returns." This is effected through the outreaches of more than 45 Derek Prince offices around the world, including primary work in Australia, Canada, China, France, Germany, the Netherlands, New Zealand, Norway, Russia, South Africa, Switzerland, the United Kingdom and the United States. For current information about these and other worldwide locations, visit www.derekprince.org.

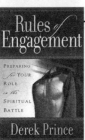
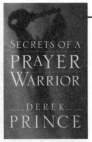
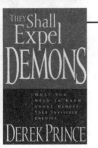

Kingdom Building Resources

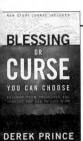

Expose the forces at work behind the everyday curses in your life so that you can experience freedom and blessing.

Blessing or Curse

Discover God's extravagant provision for all your needs as you examine what Christ truly bought at the cross.

Bought with Blood

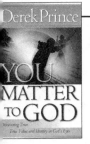

Be free from guilt, fear and shame! When you realize how incredibly loved you are, you will see life with a new vision.

You Matter to God

Discover a Prophetic Vision for the Future

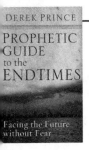

A biblically grounded and insightful guide to help you gain new understanding about what to expect as time draws to a close.

Prophetic Guide to the End Times

Chosen

www.chosenbooks.com